The Military and Denied Development in the Pakistani Punjab

Anthem Frontiers of Global Political Economy

The **Anthem Frontiers of Global Political Economy** series seeks to trigger and attract new thinking in global political economy, with particular reference to the prospects of emerging markets and developing countries. Written by renowned scholars from different parts of the world, books in this series provide historical, analytical and empirical perspectives on national economic strategies and processes, the implications of global and regional economic integration, the changing nature of the development project, and the diverse global-to-local forces that drive change. Scholars featured in the series extend earlier economic insights to provide fresh interpretations that allow new understandings of contemporary economic processes.

Series Editors
Kevin Gallagher – Boston University, USA
Jayati Ghosh – Jawaharlal Nehru University, India

Editorial Board
Stephanie Blankenburg – School of Oriental and African Studies (SOAS), UK
Ha-Joon Chang – University of Cambridge, UK
Wan-Wen Chu – RCHSS, Academia Sinica, Taiwan
Léonce Ndikumana – University of Massachusetts-Amherst, USA
Alica Puyana Mutis – Facultad Latinoamericana de Ciencias Sociales
(FLASCO-México), Mexico
Matías Vernengo – Banco Central de la República Argentina, Argentina
Robert Wade – London School of Economics and Political Science (LSE), UK
Yu Yongding – Chinese Academy of Social Sciences (CASS), China

The Military and Denied Development in the Pakistani Punjab

An Eroding Social Consensus

Shahrukh Rafi Khan and Aasim Sajjad Akhtar
with Sohaib Bodla

ANTHEM PRESS

Anthem Press
An imprint of Wimbledon Publishing Company
www.anthempress.com

This edition first published in UK and USA 2014
by ANTHEM PRESS
75–76 Blackfriars Road, London SE1 8HA, UK
or PO Box 9779, London SW19 7ZG, UK
and
244 Madison Ave #116, New York, NY 10016, USA

British Library Cataloguing-in-Publication Data
A catalogue record for this book is available from the British Library.

Library of Congress Cataloging-in-Publication Data
A catalog record for this book has been requested.

ISBN-13: 978 1 78308 289 6 (Hbk)
ISBN-10: 1 78308 289 5 (Hbk)

Cover image: Alexander Mak/Shutterstock.com and Iryna Rasko/Shutterstock.com

This title is also available as an ebook.

Dedicated to Eqbal Ahmad, inspiring activist and scholar

CONTENTS

ACKNOWLEDGMENTS

We would like to acknowledge the Eqbal Ahmad Foundation for generously providing funds for field research. We have dedicated this book to Eqbal Ahmad, because not only was he an excellent speaker, he was an equally great listener. He had the gift of making people he listened to feel special, as he heard everything they said. In that spirit, we listened to many individuals who provided material for this book. The nature of this book precludes us from listing them here, but it is they who wrote the book via their individual interviews or participation in group discussions.

We would also like to thank Zia Main, both as Vice President of the Eqbal Ahmad Foundation and for substantively and helpfully engaging with us. A fellowship from Amherst College, which facilitated the writing, and research grants from Mount Holyoke College are also gratefully acknowledged. It has been a pleasure working with Miranda Kitchener, whose efficiency we would like to acknowledge, as well as Suzanne Sherman Aboulfadl, who has worked with us on several books and has consistently done excellent work. Finally, thanks are due to Rudmila Salek for excellent and invaluable formatting assistance.

ABBREVIATIONS

BBC	British Broadcasting Corporation
BCGA	British Cotton Growing Association
BLCU	Beijing Language and Culture University
CDA	Cholistan Development Authority
CRBC	Chashma Right Bank Canal
DCO	district coordination officer
DDOR	deputy director of revenue
DG	director general
DHA	Defense Housing Authority
DOR	director of revenue
EDOR	executive director of revenue
FIR	first information report
GDP	gross domestic product
GHQ	General Headquarters
GTC	Greater Thal Canal
HQ	headquarters
IMF	International Monetary Fund
ISI	Inter-Services Intelligence
ISPR	Inter-Services Public Relations
JCO	junior commissioned officer
MI	military intelligence
MLR	martial law regulations
MNA	member of National Assembly
MQM	Mutthahida Qaumi Movement
NAB	National Accountability Bureau
NCO	noncommissioned officer
OECD	Organization for Economic Cooperation and Development
PPP	Pakistan People's Party
SHO	station house officer
TDA	Thal Development Authority
UNDP	United Nations Development Programme
WAPDA	Water and Power Development Authority

PREFACE[1]

My father was asked by a friend of his, Brigadier Ismael, if he would like to enter his name into a military General Headquarters (GHQ) lottery for a border-land distribution scheme, which was developed by Pakistan's first military dictator, Field Marshal Ayub Khan. The idea, I was told, was to give land near the Indian border to military personnel who would have the capacity to be "first responders" – or fighting men familiar with weapons and likely to have them on hand near the border – in case of enemy military action. This allocation would include noncommissioned soldiers and officers with allocation varying by seniority.

My father did not bother following up on his friend's suggestion, but Brigadier Ismael entered his name on the list anyway. My father won the lottery; his friend did not. Brigadier Ismael was later allocated land in District Sialkot, another border region. Several years passed and my father was alerted several times by GHQ to take possession of the land, but he declined to do so. Finally, he was informed by General Yahya Khan, the then army chief of general staff (later Pakistan's second military dictator with a brief tenure), to take possession or lose the land. My mother finally persuaded my father to do so, saying that his sons might one day benefit from the land. My father put half the land in my elder brother's name and half in mine.

This piece of land, roughly 60 acres, in Kasur near Mann village, three miles from the Indian border, became state property when Sikh refugees left for India. Much of the land in the area had belonged to Ranjit Singh Mann.[2] When my father first visited it with Captain Sadiq, the assistant quarter master general, it was *banjar* (or wasteland), with sand dunes, reeds and shrubs that did not seem to offer any potential for agriculture. Worst still, the two squares (*murabbas*) that were allocated to him were in bits and pieces all over the place. My father decided to take on the challenge, and his brother-in-law, Khalid Iqbal, later to be one of Pakistan's pre-eminent landscape artists, agreed to help him with the land consolidation. At that time, it took three changes of bus from Lahore to get to Mann village, from where one could walk to the land. Khalid Iqbal made the trip many times, working with the provincial land officials (*qanun go and patwaris*) who had the land records. The consolidation process was in everyone's interest, but difficult because of suspicions and difficulties in finding the relevant officials at the district level and different grades in the quality of land to be exchanged. With his congenial personality and persistence, and the clout of the military implicitly behind him, my uncle managed to have the land consolidated and made fit for agriculture.

My father's land was graded *banjar qadeem*, or waste. The 1965 war with India over Kashmir resulted in this becoming even more the case. India decided to cross the international border and start with a heavy bombardment. My father's plot of land came in for a heavy share, and when he visited it after the war the craters he saw he imagined were what a moonscape might look like.

While noncommissioned officers might generally settle on the farms as was intended, senior military officers for the most part opted for various absentee tenure relationships. My father opted for sharecropping, and a man named Kalu (literally means black) from the area became my father's first tenant. Kalu, my father told me, was a master in giving my uncle the run-around, and he eventually joined a local gang – Mann having a historic penchant for such activities.

Muhammad Rafiq, who spoke English, worked for the Water and Power Development Authority (WAPDA) as a clerk. He appeared to have much spare time on his hands and took a curious interest in my uncle. He befriended my uncle and helped him in his tireless land consolidation task, and in exchange Rafiq took over from Kalu as a sharecropper. But neither Kalu nor Rafiq offered my father much of a share, so my father decided to take matters into his own hands.

He had recently retired from the army and settled in Model Town, Lahore, about 40 miles from Kasur, where my uncle, grandmother and aunt resided. He had a small two-bedroom house with a garage and a modern bathroom, built on the land that he expected to live on when he came to oversee farming operations. His longest stay on the land was six months. He met a Pathan (from the North-West Frontier Province) laborer in Lahore, Saifur Shah, looking for work. And as a Pathan himself, my father was favorably inclined to working with him. He settled a team of Pathans on the land on a salary and he was to be the recipient of the residual income. There was never any residual income. The Pathans, sure of their inherent superiority, were out of place. They needed the cooperation of the local population – who viewed them with bemusement as aliens – but they were not really vested in making their venture, or that of my father's, a success.

The Pathans were energetic and certainly lived up to their reputation for hard work, even though it might have been misdirected. I remember once being there during harvest time and seeing them hard at work.

After the harvest, my father requested a large plate of *burfi* (a sweet confectionary of solidified condensed milk and a specialty of the area) to celebrate. This was extremely rich and I could barely get through one square inch of it. I remember marveling at how the Pathans inhaled big chunks like they were peanuts.

My father decided after his six-month stay that the farm really was not large enough to yield a sufficient income to invest all his efforts in. He had also decided that Lahore, with its very hot summers and excessively muggy monsoons, were not to his liking – Kasur was no different in this regard. He persuaded my mother to move to Islamabad, which had been created from scratch as a capital by General Ayub Khan.[3]

The chairman of the Capital Development Authority in Islamabad was trying to entice prominent senior officials to retire in the city, and plots of land were being offered at unbelievably low rates, when compared to the capital gains that were subsequently realized. My father availed the opportunity, had a house built and settled in Islamabad. He was now far removed from the land in Kasur.

After several years, my father hired a local called Inayat of the Arain caste on a fixed rent per acre basis. The people of the Arain caste are referred to admiringly as "land insects," since they are viewed to be able to do wonders with land. Inayat and his family certainly lived up to this reputation. He was a peasant par excellence. Always muddy and seemingly simple, he was sharp and understood the market very well. Over the years, he made my father invest a great deal. Initially it was one tube well, and then he himself invested in another. He had my father line the irrigation channels and help him with acquiring a tractor, for which I was the guarantor based on my share of the land.[4] He acquired other modern agricultural machinery including a tractor, a tractor trailer and a thresher. All of these he used intensively.

Inayat and his family worked hard and cultivated each inch of land that could be cultivated, including a little adjoining that belonged to the military – they got into trouble with the border Rangers for this.[5] In my many visits to the farm, carrying messages for my father, mostly about tardy payments or to demonstrate a presence or family interest, I saw how the land gradually turned into a model farm. This was also the time that my involvement with the farm increased.

I have very fond memories of these trips, which I made each time I visited family in Lahore, generally in the very hot summer. There was the usual guided trip around the land with Inayat in which I imparted messages from my father. Inayat usually informed me about his losses, the uncooperative market conditions, improvements and investments he had made and the rising cost of farming. I then had free time in which I admired the very fierce dogs, which, reassuringly, were secured by very heavy chains. These dogs announced my arrival as I drove up the dirt road to the farm house.[6] I marveled at how many flies could fit on a square inch of space on a table that contained my tea in a Thermos flask; had a cool dip in the seemingly freezing tube well tank; smiled at little children from Inayat's ever growing household; read while sitting on a *mangi* (rope bed) in the shade; and then told Inayat it was time to go. He normally joked that my trips were "hit and run" and "*jappas*" (raids). He insisted I should inform him before coming so he could make arrangements for me. I did try to leave messages, but communication was difficult with only one public telephone office in Mann at that time.

I was always amazed how quickly Inayat appeared on the land – if he was not already there when I arrived. There was a string of stalls (miscellaneous tea, sweets, machinery repair) on either side of the road that intersected the main road and led to Mann on one side and our farm on the other. My car was observed and my arrival telegraphed to Inayat, I imagine via a bicycle or pedestrian headed to the village. This was despite the fact that my car was often different depending on what I could borrow when I flew to Lahore or drove by road. The latter became more of a possibility once the motorway between Lahore and Islamabad was built: a collaborative effort between local government and Daewoo.[7]

Until the Daewoo bus service on the motorway enabled a comfortable five-hour journey (door to door), there were three options: A commercial bus journey, of about eight to nine hours on Ferozpur Road, if there were no delays; a journey of about the same time on the colonial first-class, so-called air-conditioned rail car; and air travel.[8] The car journey had many choke points when driving through the various small and larger cities along the way, and after my one and only accident, in my friend's car, I discontinued this journey. An oncoming minivan gave a turn signal and simply proceeded to turn in front of me (the oncoming traffic). Used to traffic in the West, I assumed the driver would wait until I had crossed. He was indignant that I had kept going despite his turn signal!

We made many comfortable journeys on the rail car, but getting to Islamabad's twin city, Rawalpindi, and from Lahore station to Model Town, were long journeys added to a long journey. In addition, one had to book the first-class tickets in person at the train station even though the ticket price was reasonable. My lively daughters loved the face-to-face plush, green seats (it felt like a compartment) with white head linen (Pakistan's flag colors), the large attachable tables for meals – on which crayons, reading books and all manner of coloring books were spread out – and, most importantly, being able to move up and down the aisles. My wife swore that when they made chicken sandwiches they merely passed the bread over a chicken, with very little sticking. So one had to make do with salt and pepper in soft white bread with the edges cut off. The bus journey was cramped, hot and smelly, and so a non-starter. Air travel had become too expensive and so I avoided that expense unless I could only get away for the day.

The road trip from Lahore to Kasur had three choke points and, despite the distance of only 40 kilometers, initially took about three and a half hours. The choke points included the exit from Lahore and two market towns on the way. Over time, I saw the traffic dynamics change and the travel time become shorter. This was mostly because the roads were broadened and improved, and motorized traffic of various kinds replaced pedestrians, bicycles, *tongas* (horse-drawn carriages), cattle, carts of various sorts drawn in various ways, and tractor trailers. However, the number of cars mushroomed, particularly after a Citibank executive was appointed finance minister by a military government (1999–2008). This person thought the answer to all Pakistan's economic problems was credit, and while it was nice to see many more families having access to an automobile, I saw the emissions downside as an environmentalist and the inflationary downside as an economist.

I always played John Lennon's "Imagine" in my mind when I drove through the market towns,– except I was imagining drainage and no plastic bags. There were big pools of stagnant water in front of the shops lining the roads, as one often saw outside villages, and plastic bags and containers of all colors. The organic trash emitted smells of nasty varieties and bred flies, and decayed in the hot sun. The real curse was the mosquito breeding pools and the plastic. I thought an indicator that Pakistan was making progress would be the implementation of town drainage. That did finally happen over the three decades that I traveled on that road, but a major cultural change to get good hygiene might still be decades away.

Surprisingly, I never had an accident on any one of those trips, even though I am not a slow driver and driving on those roads was often a game of chicken. My version of it was staying on the road and coming to a virtual standstill until the oncoming vehicles zoomed past, grudgingly conceding my space. Civil engineers in Pakistan do not seem to have mastered the art of making shoulders. Each time the road was re-done it was made higher and the shoulder was dirt. To my uneducated engineering mind, good gradual shoulders should protect and add life to roads, but perhaps that would defeat the purpose of securing renewed contracts.

My trips got shorter over time as the road improved, and towards the end I was back in Model Town for lunch by noon. Before, I had lunch on the farm and drove back after a rest. In the early days I even stayed the night a few times, and on one occasion I befriended Inayat's colorful brother who took me out wild boar hunting in the middle of the night. Indian dietary customs permit the eating of wild boar, which meant they were hunted and driven

THE MILITARY AND DENIED DEVELOPMENT

across Pakistan's border where eating pork is taboo.[9] The wild boar tore up the crops and so, on Inayat's request, my father provided him with a single-barrel shotgun and cartridges. Inayat's brother used to organize the hunts, and I was woken up in the middle of the night. I had decided to wear a *dhoti* (local garb), which is a rectangular wrap-around cloth. I was at the end of the line because in the excitement of a sighting, when every one ran towards the scurrying we heard (which turned out to be a porcupine), I lost my dhoti! Fortunately, I was the laggard and it was dark, but this remained one of my most memorable trips to the farm. I encouraged my family to join me, but my wife and young children, along with my aunt, only visited once.

That trip was memorable to me for several reasons. My wife is a very down-to-earth, emotionally generous and trusting woman from Peru, Indiana. For me she carried this trusting quality to a fault. She is also completely without class, and in the nuanced class society in Pakistan she communicated as an equal with all and was generally liked by all. In all our 13 years in Pakistan together, I think I can remember her distrusting only two people, and one of them was Inayat. The latter was immediately interested when my family showed up; he riddled me with questions that my wife wanted immediately translated. The gist of it was that he couldn't understand why, with two daughters, we had no intention of continuing to have offspring until we had a son. For Inayat, already the proud father of four sons, this was odd, and he more or less said I would have no one to inherit the land and carry on the family line. This discomforted my wife.

She was further discomforted when Khushi (literally means happy) Mohammed, who showed much affinity with his name, and was a constant companion and adviser of Inayat, decided to stage a show for us. He invited a local snake charmer and, after swaying, the snake was repeatedly made to strike at a cloth that the charmer waved a little too close to my family for comfort. I put an end to this, but I suspect my wife saw some symbolism in it and she never liked or trusted Inayat – and she liked Khushi even less. The latter unfortunately died of throat cancer because he loved his *hooka* (bong) too much. I was sorry not to see his cheerful face again. While I had doubts at times, particularly when payments to my father from the land stopped for prolonged periods, I basically liked Inayat and saw him as a hard worker and survivor, and as a poor man who had provided very well for his family with very hard work.

On my return from the farm, Inayat usually delayed me a little by having me collect in-season vegetables for the family in Model Town – I generally had instructions about what or what not to bring. My aunt joked about my complete lack of knowledge of the protocol of the landed gentry. She informed me that Inayat should be catering to me, serving me meals and tea, and doing my bidding unasked! Either this was not in keeping with Inayat's personality or he must have sensed my diffident and inexperienced urban ways. He sat with me on the *mungi*, rather than on the floor as other landlords might expect, referred to me as "tu" (most informal), while I referred to him as "ap" (most polite form of address in the national language, Urdu) or the equivalent in the provincial language, Punjabi, which he preferred to speak.

The basmati rice from the land was of particular good quality and my aunt looked forward to receiving half a *maund* (about 40 lb.) – the other half going to my father. Shortly after my family visited, Inayat invited me to his home for the first time, saying that the rice was there and I could drop him on my way back and pick up the rice. His house was new, *pacca* (brick) and among the most prominent in size, and, although I would not have chosen the shade of green he did, it was nice. We were seated on a chair in a room looking out on the spacious indoor courtyard. I was surprised that shortly after, a young and very pretty woman appeared from the courtyard (Inayat's eldest daughter), without a shawl or *dupatta*, with a sack of rice which she started separating into two halves in a businesslike manner in front of us. I was surprised because it is most unusual for a young woman to appear without cover in front of a stranger in a Muslim household. Shortly after, Inayat stopped growing rice because he argued the sandy soil soaked up too much of his water.

Inayat continued to be late with payments, which he attributed to the vagaries of the weather or fickleness of the market. Sometimes my father decided to forego the payments, but he did at least finally start receiving some payments. He was a good landlord in the sense that he did respond to the tenant's call for appropriate investments, and he had the clout to make changes happen when called for.

For example, one unfortunate investment my father made was in a guava and mango orchard. The market price had skyrocketed and at the time it seemed like a good investment. Also, my father was very fond of fruit trees – they were in abundance in our own home in Islamabad. He loved to supervise the planting of gardens; fruit blossoms were among his favorite joys. Thus, guava and mango trees were planted on a large part of the farm. As the guava trees matured the market price of guavas collapsed, since many farmers followed the same advice of getting trouble-free income. The Kasur land had sandy soil that was most unsuited for mangoes and so the mango trees were not a good investment either. He had a white elephant on his hands that looked good but delivered little economically. This irked Inayat, who fretted over better uses for this land. My father discovered that, while the land was his, the condition of the land allocation was that any tree planted belonged to the army for sheltering tanks during war. It was an arduous task to secure permission to remove the orchard, especially considering he retired as a senior general in the army from the influential post of military secretary to the president.

My brother and I were both uncomfortable with the notion of being absentee owners and finally persuaded our father to sell the land in 2006. He had kept the rental much lower than was being paid in the area, but even then late payments, deferred payments and forgiven payments were frequent – this worked in our favor. We also knew that extensive water emissions from the leather tanning industry, that were collecting in pools outside Kasur and on the way to Mann, were seeping into the ground water and that this might eventually impact the value of the land. While capital gains could be realized if the land was declared an urban municipality, and Kasur was expanding fast, we reasoned that the same capital invested in land near the capital would appreciate even faster.

We were also concerned because at least half the cultivation was (rightly) being recorded in Inayat's name by the local land revenue officials (*patwaris*) and this would eventually give the tiller ownership rights. My brother had first noticed this and tried to change it, as is common practice, so that cultivation was recorded in our name, but with only partial success. While as an academic I completely support the so-called land to the tiller position, on grounds of efficiency and social justice, I did not follow through on my principles by foregoing ownership rights to this piece of land. While Inayat was illiterate, he knew the system well and I believed he was shrewd and not beyond using it to his advantage.

My attempts to get the documentation changed exposed me to the offices of the local government and courts. It is no wonder that the Swatis initially favored the quick and speedy justice of the Taliban – though the ruthless and cruel bullying changed their minds. Negotiating the miscellaneous traffic in Mann was the first nightmare, and invariably the *patwari* would be away from his home and office. I think Inayat finally took pity, and we found the *patwari*, but the procedure of recording cultivation, he explained, was complicated, involved being present at the right time and involved going to the courts. I followed up in the courts as best as I could, and I realized just how powerful local government and judicial officials were in their own domain. I seemed to have honorary status and was able to get access to offices because of my association with my father (which became less important over time because he was retired) and because I was from Islamabad (the capital city) with a vague and hard to understand affiliation on my business card. I got the benefit of the doubt by acting suitably unintimidated. But despite my brother's and my efforts, the records only changed sporadically.

I informed Inayat, based on my father's decision to sell the land, of the current market price, and that he had first right of refusal either individually or in partnership with another party. Inayat by this time had built a huge water pond on the land with almost 60 happy water buffalos in it (each then conservatively priced at 100,000 rupees).[10] Thus, I suspected that, notwithstanding his simple appearance, he might have accumulated substantial capital. Inayat first tried to persuade me against the sale. He argued that selling land was extremely dishonorable and used local proverbs to seal the argument. In fact, he had been actively trying to persuade us to buy the land across the brick road that had come up for sale. Since we had raised the possibility of sale earlier, it seems he did not take us seriously.

However, we proceeded with the sale, which was no easy task. Much of the burden, as had happened before when I left for the USA in 1986 (I returned in 1993), fell on my brother, as I accepted a teaching position in the USA in 2002. On my brother's intervention, one that I supported, my sister was first given a one-fifth share of the land, in accordance with Islamic law (the brothers each getting two-fifths), which was then was raised to one-third. This brought in another party (resident at that time in France) to the transaction, but one also supporting the sale. The military bureaucracy, like most, is daunting. Were it not for the respect my father commanded in military circles, getting a no objection certificate (NOC) for sale from General Headquarters in Rawalpindi may have been very difficult and may have taken much longer than the years it took.

I remember sitting in the office of the colonel of the Border Area Committee in Lahore with buyers when one transaction went very badly wrong. We had agreed to a price and the quantity of land with a professor of agricultural studies at Pakistan's most prominent agricultural university. I never was able to find him on the website, but took his claim at face value. During the transaction, he and his son proceeded to reduce the prior quoted price because my father was no longer in possession of the twin urban settlement in Mann that had been part of the initial allocation for settlement purposes. The wife of one of his close friends had taken possession and my father did not contest this. However, the documentation in the Border Area Committee office in Lahore showed the *marlas* belonging to my father. When my brother and I stuck to the original quote, the transaction turned into a one-sided shouting match. We remained calm and refused the offer, and fortunately the colonel supported our right to do so, especially as we had the papers documenting ownership. We had arrived in the car of the buyers who had picked us up and so they dropped us back to Model Town. They very quickly seemed to get over their anger and it became evident from their conversation that they were land dealers who were currently engaged in many other land transactions. My father's two conditions for the sale were: no land dealers and no token money. They had fooled us regarding not being dealers, and my father's refusal to accept a token payment saved us from complications.

After many missteps, shady buyers and false starts, a trustworthy buyer was finally secured. It was very reassuring that it was finally Inayat who found a buyer. This was a relief for two reasons: First, because we all wanted Inayat to be comfortable with the sale; and second, we all wanted his continued livelihood on the farm secured. As a practical matter, this would also mean that the buyer would find getting possession easy, and we were all concerned about the possibility of ugly incidents if the land passed into the wrong party's hands. They all seemed so nice and trustworthy on first contact! The sale of the land partially provided the capital for me to put a down payment on a house in Stamford, Connecticut, and for my sister, an artist, to build a beautiful house on a small farm in the outskirts of Islamabad (earlier purchased jointly with my brother).

The story of this piece of land is simple and one perhaps often repeated with variations. It is not a story in which I stuck to my long held academic beliefs. I have consistently opposed absentee ownership and capital flight as a development economist, and yet I was party to both. However, as a development economist, I realized there was a fascinating set of broader issues revolving around the story of this piece of land. In particular, these included the military's role in the agrarian economy and society. After thinking about these issues for many years, I contacted Aasim Sajjad Akhtar who also had an interest in these issues and we started looking for research support. We received a small grant from the Eqbal Ahmed Foundation to conduct fieldwork, and our conceptualizations of the issue and the findings of the fieldwork are the subject of the rest of this book.

The pre-test for the fieldwork was conducted in Kasur early in the summer of 2009, and so I was able to see how Inayat's story unfolded. The trip to Kasur from Lahore took 27 minutes because the wider double-lane Ferozpur Road had been extended to the border. The road and relative peace caused the land prices and rental contracts to increase ten-fold from when we had sold it. I was delighted to meet Inayat who, in effect, said, "I told you so"; he did not believe me when I told him I had no regrets. He had taken the loss of one young son at 18 to a heart attack very hard and insisted he had aged, though he looked good to me. His simple appearance had not changed, but his prosperity was evident in the way his sons dressed and carried themselves, the motorcycles they rode, the cell phones they carried, and the seed shop they managed. His former associates, from when I visited the farm regularly, now had a deferential manner towards him. While he had not been allowed to continue as the tenant on my father's farm, the new owner had allowed him to cultivate another of his farms, 32 acres in size. He also still cultivated my father's friend's farm of 150 acres that adjoined his eight acre farm. So whilst he did not have the 60 buffaloes (very high maintenance), he appeared to be doing very well.

Apart from the two-lane road, Kasur's other major improvement was the result of a comprehensive effluent treatment project including a joint effluent treatment facility – funded by the provincial and federal government, the United Nations Development Programme (UNDP) and the United Nations Industrial Development Organization (UNIDO) – that drained the ponds of toxic wastes from the leather tanneries. I am pleased to report that my fear of land depreciation due to the poisoning of the ground water is no longer an issue. However, whilst there seems to have been progress, the military's involvement in Pakistan's economy generally, and agrarian society more specifically, is a structural issue that calls out for exploration, since Pakistan's intermittent democracy is unlikely to be sustained without a clear understanding of such issues.

I am fortunate to have found in Aasim Sajid Akhtar and Sohaib Riaz Bodla: two dedicated and committed researchers to explore these issues with me. One has been trained in economics and sociology and the other in anthropology, and their insights combine well with my training as an economist. However, we share the view of other scholars that disciplinary boundaries are arbitrary and view the research that led to this book as inter- and multidisciplinary social science.

This preface narrates a personal story. As a social scientist I am aware that this need not accord with the general story on this issue of land allocations to military personnel. In fact, this story suggests a very benign view of military land allocations compared to the stories of military land allocations presented next and in more detail in chapters 4 and 5.

In Rakh Azizabad and Rakh Sadiqabad (situated near Chowk Munda, District Rajin Pur) 30,000 acres of the land was allotted to in-service and retired army personnel in 2007. Many farmers had been cultivating this land for more than a century. The farmers reported that the allotment army men, accompanied by the police, started to displace them. The farmers collectively resisted giving possession. Army officials who managed to occupy land subsequently sold it. Others continued to try to occupy it with the support of the police, and met with much resistance, so much so, that the protests were highlighted by leading newspapers (*Daily Khabrain*, *Nawaiwakt* and *Jang Multan* on 2 July 2008 and *Daily Dawn* on 20 March 2009).

In union council Fateh Pur the air force personnel were allotted 335 acres of mainly agricultural land in 2001. Without prior notice, the land, houses and shops of the local people cultivating and living on the land was bulldozed. People protested and took their complaints to the civilian officials but were not compensated for the land they had been cultivating for decades, and those leading the protest were arrested.

In Rakh Kona, Tehsil Chobara and District Layyah, 20,500 acres of land were allotted to the military in 1982–83 for a pittance of 146 rupees per acre, to be paid in installments over 20 years. In Rakh Jaded of the same *tehsil*, 40,000 acres were allotted. The senior officers installed large boards as markers of ownership. Much of this land has been contracted out for cultivation or sold at market prices. As usual, the land had been made cultivatable by locals and their protests were unheeded.

In pursuing these stories our work follows up on the work of Siddiqa (2007) who exhaustively mapped the Pakistani military's commercialization, its welfare programs, activity of its foundations, its land holdings and its role in the economy.[11] We explore one aspect of this involvement in agrarian society and economy in more detail, since this aspect of her work is not as detailed as the rest. Whilst the value of agricultural plots is a pittance compared to residential plots, which we also briefly explore in chapter 6, agricultural allocations also bring forth interesting historical, institutional, political, sociological and economic issues, which we explore in this book. A brief synopsis of the book follows.

In chapter 1 we review the concept of economic development and, in that context, explore the role of Pakistan's military. We turn next to an illustrative comparative performance of Pakistan's economy under military compared to civilian administrations. We show that there is little justification for military intervention on economic grounds.

We follow up by drawing on the literature to make a more detailed case for democracy as preferable to military governments for development and more broadly. Finally, we reflect on the military mindset that perpetuates its rapacious behavior and creates social resentment, hence undermining its effectiveness.

The thesis in this book is that, apart from the raw power, the military has been able to rely on a base of support in the Punjab province. This support was premised on a number of interrelated factors, which we highlight in chapter 2. We argue that a significant cross section of Punjabi society has either directly or indirectly been co-opted into a military-dominated political economy. Given that Pakistan's military, including paramilitary forces and reserves, is now about a million strong, a great deal of economic activity is generated through various multiplier effects and therefore a sizeable proportion of the labor force is absorbed.

We argue in this chapter that this base of support is eroding, that there is a growing public perception that the military has over reached and that the social costs of its economic empire building exceed the social benefits, even in the Punjab province. The lawyer-led movement against the General Musharraf regime is one manifestation of such erosion, but we argue that this goes much deeper and that the military will find it increasingly difficult to appropriate an asymmetrical and inequitable share of state resources and the commons.

To establish exactly how the state–society consensus in Punjab may be breaking down, we review the imperatives of the colonial army and the post-colonial state. Following that, we discuss the creation and evolution of the security state after partition. We review the military's agricultural land allocations and the responses to these allocations. Finally, we argue that there was a consensus on the security state, and in the rest of the book demonstrate that the consensus is breaking down and the military is no longer being perceived as a guardian.

In chapter 3, we start by explaining our research design – and how it evolved – and method. We turn next to the institutional issues pertinent to our research, including the conceptualization of the military land allotment scheme; the allocation process; legal issues, including those pertaining to civil-military conflict; and border Rangers and police jurisdiction issues. We end by providing information on the scope of the border and nonborder allocations.

In chapter 4, we first provide an account of the nature of military land acquisitions in the border belt and in the non-border area. In each case, our focus is on the perceptions of the locals who experience this intervention on a daily basis. In our view, there is an amazing amount of similarity and consistency in the stories we heard all across the border region. We also extensively document the predatory practices of the border Rangers. We show that the predation at the macro level is replicated on the micro level.

In chapter 5, we document the social resentment and resistance resulting from the military's land acquisitions. We have organized this chapter by area and in the order in which our fieldwork progressed. As in chapter 4, we narrate what we gleaned from several sources using key informants and group discussions, although fact checking in all cases was not possible. The perceptions that we document are important in that they contribute to social resistance and social movements.

Chapters 6 and 7 are detailed case studies. In chapter 6, following the research method adopted for chapters 4 and 5, we document the military's involvement in real estate business in the peri-urban areas and how this has led to social injustice. Chapter 7 explores, in detail, the most well-known case of peasant resistance to the military as a landlord, which occurred in Okara, Punjab in 2000. This case study draws on earlier work and is self-contained. However, it is consistent with the main themes of the book: military predation and social resistance. In addition, it ties together other themes of historical development and state theory that we introduce as a conceptual framework for the book in chapter 2.

The final chapter summarizes the main findings of the book. In a nutshell, the military's resource acquisitions, in general and of land in particular, amount to development denied. The more resources the military draws based on its power, the less there is for the rest of society to invest in human, social and physical infrastructure; industrialization; and social and environmental safeguards. In this book, we document that there is less and less patience for this state of affairs – even in the Punjab province, where its base of support was the strongest – and that social resistance to the military's predatory behavior has begun to emerge.

Notes

1 This preface is written by Shahrukh Rafi Khan. Given my training as a development economist, making some observations emanating from this training was inevitable. I have relegated these to endnotes to avoid impeding the narrative written for the general reader.

2 Ranjit Singh Mann (1799–1839) was a Sikh maharaja.

3 General Ayub Khan viewed the port city Karachi as both the seat of national government and the financial and business center of the country, as militarily insecure, and prone to corruption. He viewed Islamabad as more isolated, and therefore militarily secure, and a place that ensured a distant and professional association between the economic bureaucracy and businessmen.

4 It was this transaction that showed me the connection between poor tax administration and corruption. Essentially, the state collects very little in revenue and so has left the citizens at the mercy of the bureaucracy to collect their own specific taxes for specific services. When I went into the local agricultural development bank in Kasur to collect an application form for the tractor, I was informed that none were available. Inayat, who knew local ways and how to bend to them, told me to wait outside. He returned in a minute with a form and informed me there was a "fee" to be paid. All services had an earmarked "fee." When I returned with the completed application, the bank official looked very sheepish but explained that he commutes from Lahore and that his salary would not even cover commuting costs. He was very friendly, gave me his card, wrote his personal address and phone number on the back, and invited me to visit him. This was all to establish that there should be no hard feelings and that we merely engaged in a routine transaction. Perhaps, but it still felt like an uncomfortable initiation to me.

5 Border rangers feature very prominently in this book from chapter three onwards.

6 To get to the farm, I drove down Ferozpur Road towards Kasur. Past Kasur, about three miles short of the Indian border, there was an intersecting brick/dirt road (in very bad condition) leading to Mann village, where Inayat lived with his family in a spunky new house. Turning left, rather than right towards the village, led to the Bambawali Ravi Bedian (BRB) irrigation canal (shortly after which is the Indian border again). A few hundred yards short of the canal, past the *mazar* (shrine) on the right, is a dirt road perpendicular to the brick road. It turns left 100 yards in at a right angle and moves parallel to the brick road up to the farmhouse. Since the land is very flat, the small farmhouse, trees and the larger animals are visible after the *mazar*.

7 This is better constructed and maintained than most motorways I have seen in the West, and it's exceptionally policed. It is an amazing demonstration of effective foreign and local partnership between a foreign company (Daewoo) and local government, and also of how functioning institutions can be created against the odds. A special police force was created and trained with a much higher salary structure. They are courteous, but not even a member of parliament is spared a ticket. So effective has this police force

been that they were invited to police the capital with a remarkable transformation of traffic discipline from a free-for-all to one that is watchful and disciplined. Transparency International declared the Islamabad Tariff Police corruption free in 2009 (*Daily Times* A3). The Daewoo bus services (economy and luxury) are also a marvel of economy, efficiency, safety and punctuality. All the security protocols of air travel are carried out but they take much less time. Thus the door-to-door time for the two alternatives is almost equivalent despite the fact that the actual flying time between the two cities is only 35 minutes. This makes bus travel a reasonable and much cheaper alternative. As economist Joseph Schumpeter's theory predicts, there was entry into the market by copycats, but the diffusion of business and managerial practices are slow and the Daewoo brand still has luster after almost two decades of operation.

8   This is the same road that goes on after Lahore to Kasur. It is also called the Grand Trunk Road and was built by the emperor Sher Shah Suri in the sixteenth century. It traverses Pakistan and goes across India and on to Bangladesh. This road has now been turned into a dual carriageway with many bypasses. It still does not match the motorway in speed, though it is a more direct route and hence shorter.

9   I heard from Inayat's brother that on the Sialkot border the rangers on either side made regular exchanges of wild boar for wild beast. The Pakistanis hunted the wild beast and drove it to the Indian side, where they were relatively safer because of Hindu dietary taboos.

10   The exchange rate at this time in 2001 was about 60 rupees for one US dollar.

11   Seemingly batting for the Pakistani military, Cloughley (2008) claims that Siddiqa (2007) makes allegations without supporting evidence (see chapter six).

References

Cloughley, B. 2008. *War, Coups, & Terror: Pakistan's Army in Years of Turmoil.* New York: Skyhorse Publishing.

Siddiqa, A. 2007. *Military Inc.: Inside Pakistan's Military Economy.* Karachi: Oxford University Press.

Chapter One

THE MILITARY AND ECONOMIC DEVELOPMENT IN PAKISTAN[1]

Introduction

The survival and flourishing of civilian rule in Pakistan, which is now and is likely to remain critically important for the foreseeable future, requires a fundamental reordering of the balance of power between state institutions, and between state and society. The military establishment has for the most part dominated a zero-sum game of accumulating power.[2] Political elites have at times collaborated with the military for short-term advantages to the detriment of democracy. Over time more and more power – political but also economic – has been ceded to the military. This power has grown not only during military takeovers, that have given the military formal control of all organs of the state, but also via the pressure the military has exercised during the rule of civilian governments in the shaping of policy and influencing budget allocations. More broadly, military power has grown due to the military's increasing economic autonomy so that its dependence on elected government has lessened over time.

The source of this power has partially been based on allowing the various arms of the military to build business empires and ceding large tracts of real estate to their control. Our premise is that the more economic autonomy the military gains, the less answerable it is to civilian oversight, a key prerequisite to sustainable democracy in Pakistan. Furthermore, the more economic power it gains, the larger the threat democratic oversight represents since the stakes are higher.

This is an application of the theory of coups put forward by Acemoglu and Robinson (2006) where the dominant elite (the military) defends its privileges by co-opting other dominant groups, including feudal, industrial, bureaucratic and judicial elites, to periodically stage coups. Bhave and Kingston (2010) extend this game-theoretic model to cater specifically to Pakistan's unique history. Historical and institutional theories of coups, as summarized by Cohen (1994, 107–117), emphasize political vacuums, ambitious generals, foreign policy concerns, foreign interests and Punjabi domination. Aziz's (2008) thesis is that all the coups in Pakistan, including the first one in 1958, resulted from the military seeking to protect and extend its institutional interests, including the economic.

An essential step in ensuring oversight over the military is exploring and revealing the full nature of its involvement in various sectors of the economy and its ability to use its political muscle to gain economic advantage, hence perpetuating militarism and undermining democracy. This is imperative if there is to be success in gradually paring back the military's special privileges and establishing more equity across the services, civil and military, based on a reasonable assessment of resource constraints.

Senior military officers enjoy an exalted status in society and are accustomed to a very high standard of living. If all perks and subsidies are monetized, the real salary of the top brass is very high. Retirement means a loss of status but also, in many cases, a very big drop in living standards when they reach their mid-fifties – active years for most. This is the crux of the problem that political governments have to deal with. Military foundations such as Fauji, Shaheen and Baharia allow officers to sustain a higher living standard and status into their retirement years, but their survival is dependent on subsidies. Sustaining large welfare programs is inefficient if based on subsidies, unjust if not sanctioned by people's representatives and inequitable if they exceed those of other public functionaries and the constraints imposed by the economy.

Another mechanism for building and sustaining economic dominance by the military is systematic land grabbing, which can be traced back to the colonial period. Under the British, land grants to retired military personnel were considered a means of ensuring loyalty and therefore social peace, particularly in Punjab, which provided the bulk of the military's rank and file after about 1880 (see chapter 2 for more details).[3] This land grab has now been transformed into a social welfare program to ensure a comfortable retirement for officers, particularly senior military officers, and the economic future of their progeny.

While the military is not the only institution in Pakistan that makes a rapacious and disproportionate grab for resources, there are reasons to focus on the military. First, its power means it can be much more effective in grabbing resources. Second, the press at least is willing to shed some light on the rent-seeking behavior of the civil bureaucracy and political elites. The military is much too powerful an institution, and journalists perceive the consequences of crossing generals and brigadiers too severe to scrutinize military affairs rigorously. Third, there is a lack of transparency in military transactions as the relevant data are routinely stated to be confidential. And that is expected to be the end of the story.

The Pakistani military is not unique in its economic interventionism and its command over national resources. However, as we will document, it may exceed others in the extent to which it draws on the national budget. Firat (2005) documents a commercial role played by the Turkish military, and Dobell (2003, 5) claims that only 30 percent of Indonesia's military expenditure comes from the budget, i.e., is subject to parliamentary oversight; the rest comes from commercial enterprises and a great deal of illegal activity. Cloughley (2008, 145) points out that the Indian Army also engages in welfare activities for its soldiers, although it enjoys far less autonomy than its Pakistani counterpart.

In the rest of this chapter, we first review some general conceptions of economic growth and development and then apply them to the Pakistani case. We turn next to the performance of Pakistan's economy under military, compared to civilian, administrations. We show that there is little justification for military intervention on economic grounds. Finally, we reflect on the military mindset that perpetuates its rapacious behavior, creates social resentment and hence gives rise to conflict.

Economic Growth and the Development Process

Poor countries strive to catch up with rich ones, but the task is very challenging. In Pakistan's case, the military adds to this challenge in several obvious and less obvious ways. They are highlighted in this chapter. We start out with some reflections on China – widely depicted as the latest miracle economy – and see what lessons the Chinese experience might offer for an economy featuring an overbearing military burden and numerous political and social conflicts.

Over the past seven decades or so, scholars have identified many factors that might break vicious circles that lead to low economic growth and initiate a high and sustained economic growth trajectory – governance being among the more recent ones.[1] However, as Hausmann, Klinger and Wagner (2008, 5–16) conclude when making a case for growth diagnostics, all approaches to identifying constraints to growth – such as cross-country growth regressions, growth accounting or benchmarking using cross-country surveys, in which countries are ranked on various indicators such as constraints to doing business – are problematic. These methods are dismissed on theoretical grounds and in the case of benchmarking because of inherent problems with the data collection method. However, as indicated by Dixit (2007), growth diagnostics, the latest in the arsenal of such tools, is also problematic on many grounds. Case studies have been more promising; one lesson is that there is no one solution for moving from vicious to virtuous circles, and certainly, countries that have managed to attain and sustain a high economic growth trajectory have had very different points of origin and proceeded in very different ways.

Rostow (1960) reflected on the preconditions for economic take-off. While he ostensibly wrote an anticommunist manifesto, his stages-of-growth framework is not unlike that implicit in Mao Tse-tung's thought. Rostow describes preconditions for take-off as the critical stage prior to economic take-off. These preconditions include a change in attitude to fundamental and applied science and training to operate in disciplined organizations. Other preconditions include the development of financial, political and social institutions. Institutional development needs to be accompanied by appropriate social and physical infrastructure (ports, docks, roads, railways) and management skills.

Mao Tse-tung's (1968, 5, 67) characterization of a take-off would be quantification and then a qualitative leap, where the quantification is the precondition and the take-off the qualitative leap. Mao Tse-tung also refers to internal and external conditions, with the former, as the precondition, being more critical (1968, 28) and external conditions, such as a favorable international environment, possibly acting as a catalyst. A take-off, or whatever one calls the phenomenon (catch-up growth), is an empirical reality in the case of China and perhaps other emerging economies like Brazil and India. This was certainly the case in Japan, Korea and Taiwan, and Malaysia and Thailand before them.

Mao appears to be right in suggesting that qualitative changes matter greatly, but we do not know as much about what causes them and why, at least relative to the quantitative steps that are taken first. It is also the case, as we noted earlier, that the critical internal and external conditions vary significantly by country. We speculate in this chapter on what the critical internal conditions are likely to be in Pakistan's case.

We first make a qualification given our concern with social justice. A take-off is not a necessary condition for generalized wellbeing, as we are currently seeing in China and India, although it is a sufficient condition. A take-off can create opportunities for distribution and pressures for it. The more likely story is that prosperity spreads because people fight for a larger share of the larger pie (e.g. worker strikes in China); or the state engages in distribution because of the likely social conflict and other constraints to growth if they do not (e.g., China addressing lagging rural income with infrastructure). Nor do workers necessarily wait for a sustained take off. Bangladeshi ready-made garment workers have been engaged in a protracted struggle for increased wages from a sector that contributes over about four-fifths of total merchandize export earnings. Just as nations have to struggle and develop despite the odds, workers often face a similar struggle.

In the context of Mao's philosophy, among the very favorable internal conditions are a sound administration and managerial capacity and strong citizen identification with a common national project. One of the authors of this book made a trip to China to give a series of lectures on economic development in the summer of 2009, during the peak of the swine flu pandemic, at the Beijing Language and Culture University (BLCU). It was strange to be lecturing on economic development in a country that one really should be learning from. In fact, one lesson, pertaining to administrative and managerial capacity, came very early on in the trip even before reaching the hotel from the airport. On disembarking in Islamabad, Pakistan, en route to China, passengers were greeted with a large sign suggesting that they report to the Ministry of Health if they were coming from a country where the flu originated or where the incidence was high. The best that can be said for this public-health initiative was that the sign was prominent and difficult to miss. It seems unlikely, however, that many passengers would have reported to the Ministry of Health the next day. Two days later, when the plane landed in China, the public-health precaution could not have been more different. When the plane came to a complete stop, passengers were asked to remain seated. Rapidly and carefully, a team of public-health officials electronically scanned each passenger's temperature. Seat numbers of those with a temperature above a certain threshold were noted, and these passengers were later subjected to further tests. We learned that day that the mayor of New Orleans was quarantined for a week in a Shanghai hotel because he was deemed to represent a risk to public health. In the case of BLCU, foreign faculty members were not allowed to be exposed to students for one week, during which time sightseeing tours were organized (to which families, if in tow, were also invited, board and lodging covered).

Other experiences also revealed a very high level of public health alert and the capacity to take preventive measures across the board. Taxi drivers routinely opened windows if a passenger sneezed, suggesting an effective public health campaign. In Qingdao, 882 km south of Beijing on the Yellow Sea, a family member's sore throat bloomed into a cold. Medicine for a cold was procured from a traditional medicine store by looking at a visual card showing apparent cold symptoms. A hotel receptionist with English language skills was asked to read the dosage. Very shortly after, a public-health official knocked at our hotel room door for a temperature check.

All this precaution for public health was very visible to a foreigner in Chinese society without knowledge of the language. More might have been gleaned with access to the language and media. Even so, the level of preparedness regarding public health, both at the official level and in terms of the diffusion of knowledge, possibly via media campaigns, was impressive.

Perhaps it is the administrative and managerial ability of the communist party that generates the observed level of efficiency. However, as observers and interested readers of the Chinese scene, it also appears that there is a broad identification with what one might view as a common project to catch up with the West as soon as possible. Insofar as development is a collective action issue, this critical ingredient for a collective action to be realized seems to be present in China.

A country as vast as China is inevitably complex; many people are shabbily treated and human rights appear to be trampled on. But there seems to be a larger story of a country on the move, a country that possesses adequate administrative and managerial capacity, a country where there is broad identification with a national project.

These two critical ingredients may be sufficient to trigger a virtuous circle by inducing other ingredients that add to the snowballing impact of enhanced economic prosperity. For example, one way to look at the current Chinese miracle is that, historically, the administrative and managerial ability delivered reasonable quality physical and social infrastructure as a base. That this happened was no accident; it was systematically planned for in the dialectical vision of economic development and balanced growth that Mao Tse-tung (1968, 129–130) propounded in 1951. Heavy industry was to be the core, but it required the simultaneous development of agriculture and the associated light industry. Agriculture would provide the raw materials and markets and enable the capital accumulation needed for heavy industry. In turn, industry would provide materials needed to continue to boost agriculture such as heavy machinery and transportation equipment, fertilizer, equipment for water conservancy, power, fuel, and building materials for infrastructure.

A managerial decision to catch up with the West then put uniquely Chinese incentives into place to trigger prosperity (Rodrik, 2010); again, very consistent with Mao's advocacy of adaptation based on local conditions (Mao, 131). The original source of the organizational and managerial ability might have been the communist party, which is still a force, but this ability is widely diffused; visiting any factory or observing the cleanliness and efficiency of the subway systems in Beijing or Shanghai makes this evident.[5]

Finally, to sustain prosperity and truly catch up with the West, a country is required to embody an endogenous technological capacity in society and the economy; this way, it can keep moving up the technological ladder (Chang 2010). However, as the Japanese, Korean and Taiwan experience shows, this is not automatic but planned for with an extensive technology and training policy (Gallagher and Shafaeddin 2010). Now, it is also evident that the Chinese are using their newfound resources and administrative and managerial ability to invest in creating an endogenous technological capacity; this includes drawing back expatriate talent (LaFraniere 2010; Zweig 2006).

However, China faces major challenges. As mentioned above, the socialist investment in humans, as the ultimate wealth of the nation, and infrastructure created the base for the unleashing of China's productive potential as it harnessed the power of the market. Deng Xiaoping, the architect of market reforms, is alleged to have said, "To get rich is Glorious." Despite this unleashing of personal incentives, the state has not withdrawn from continuing to make human investments. And as a medium human development nation, its human development index increased from 0.556 in 1985 to 0.772 in 2007. However, social inequality has increased, and while the Gini coefficient in 1981 was 28.8, it rose to 38.8 in 1995 and to 45.0 in 2001.[6]

The Communist Party of China leadership seems to have recognized this problem, as is evident from statements during a plenary meeting of the party's Central Committee. This might have accounted for the drop in the most recent Gini coefficient to 41.5 (UNDP 2009, 196).[7] The Communist Party of China also recognized that industrialization was resulting in immense environmental degradation and human suffering and its current drive to lead in renewable technologies like solar and wind might have been one response to this immense challenge. Its metric tons of CO_2 per thousand dollars of GDP declined from 1.77 in 1990 to 0.95 in 2005: the steepest decline among all countries for which such data were reported (World Bank 2010, 262).

Thus, authentic development for us requires investing in people as an end, but also as a means for attaining equitable and sustained prosperity by developing an endogenous technological capacity to diversify the economy. Such capacity needs to be harnessed, along with containing consumption, to preserve natural capital. While China's centralized leadership may have advantages in its capacity to deliver on such objectives, our preferences incline strongly towards democratic methods and institutions, and so we would be averse to recommending centralized and autocratic practices to deliver administrative and managerial capacity.

In Pakistan's case, there is one institution that does seem to have the administrative and managerial capacity to deliver as indicated above for China. Based on the traditions of the British colonial military, the Pakistani military distances itself from the population, physically and otherwise. This may be necessary to inculcate and preserve an administrative and managerial capacity that enables it to get things done efficiently. All who have exposure to the military cantonments and bases testify to the quality of maintenance. Resources certainly help, but resources can leak via corruption or improper use without delivering much.

However, such administrative and managerial capacity and efficiency is not unique to the military. Indeed, the better managed private sector firms and universities show similar excellence, as do Pakistan's motorway police.

One could argue that such capacity was devoted to developing and sustaining a nuclear program (Pakistan's equivalent of a space race), although in our view the country would have been better served had this single-minded effort been directed towards a drive to eliminate illiteracy. While the military's evident managerial and administrative superiority is widely accepted among the educated public and part of popular lore, the key questions for us are whether this capacity is real – can or should it be tapped for broader economic development? – and whether the military represents a constraint to economic development in Pakistan. Let us consider a possible diffusion mechanism of the military's superior administrative and managerial ability.

The military could directly engage in economic activities and diffuse its success to the private sector in a competitive framework. However, the cost effectiveness, or profitability, of this activity is difficult to gauge because of a lack of access to the data needed for evaluation. Indeed, judging from the need to bail out commercial military operations with subsidies, it seems much more likely that the military is not competitive in private sector activity (Siddiqa 2007, ch. 9). A prominent English-language daily newspaper, *The News International*, on 22 September 2010 quoted a report by the Parliament Public Accounts Committee stating that the military run corporations were drawing an annual subsidy of 200 billion Pakistan rupees. This was about half the budgeted Public Sector Development Program of Rs406 billion for 2009–10 (Government of Pakistan 2010, 39).

Many, of these corporations are headed and staffed by retired military personnel. One could argue that they carry their discipline into these activities after retirement and this should contribute to success. But private sector activities are complex and require more than military training. This could account for the high failure rate of military ventures into economic activities. As of yet, there is no compelling case to support the military's venture in private sector activity.

The military's other forays into civilian life, that could have diffused a sense of discipline and efficiency, have been no more successful. Retired military personal in civil society organizations bring to their work some of the strengths of their military training. However, discipline, punctuality and carrying out instructions efficiently are offset by a lack of flexibility and creativity. There is also a cultural clash between democratic norms and their autocratic and hierarchical mindset.

General Pervez Musharraf made the standard arrogant assumption held in the military that uniformed personnel are better than civilians in all matters and appointed serving generals to head important civil institutions, including the Pakistan Cricket Board.[8] The Water and Power Development Authority (WAPDA), one of the largest utilities in the country, was put under the management of a serving general in 1999. The average annual power and distribution losses for the next five years (until 2003) increased to 25.7 percent of total output relative to 23.0 percent during the political governments (see table 1.2). The general's disastrous tenure as the head of cricket in Pakistan caused much heartache.

Thus, Pakistan's sustained take-off is unlikely to be based on the kind of administrative and managerial capacity described for China, and the military certainly cannot be relied upon to diffuse such a capacity by militarizing civilian life each time it assumes dictatorial power and arrests the political process. With each suspension of the political process, military personnel have made deeper inroads into civilian life, not in the greater national interest, but in the interest of sustaining a growing military economic empire whose beneficiaries are military personnel and their families rather than the general public.

Is the Military's Economic Management in Pakistan More Efficient?

We have argued above that the administrative and managerial capacity that the military uses to handle its affairs does not translate as success in private sector activities, administering public corporations or in running civil society organizations. Nonetheless, there is a widely held assumption in the military that it can much more competently manage the economy. The lack of civilian competence in this regard was stated by General Musharraf as one of the reasons for assuming power in much the same way as the three other intervening generals before him. Serving generals were not appointed in key economic positions, but it was assumed that the military administration would have the judgment to appoint competent people to improve economic performance.

There is no simple way to test the economic performance of a military administration and compare it with that of a civilian administration. Comparing the administration of General Ayub Khan (1958–69) with those that preceded or followed it might be a good test case, because he was personally involved in economic management. His Political Autobiography, *Friends Not Masters*, suggests a vision of development not unlike that of President Park Chung-hee (1961–79) of the Republic of Korea. The two countries had a similar GDP per capita in the 1950s. Pakistan's GDP per capita as a percentage of the US GDP per capita in 1950 and 1960 was 9 percent and 7.8 percent respectively, while the Republic of Korea's was 7.6 percent (lower than Pakistan's) and 11.8 percent respectively. By 1995, this percentage was still stagnant at 8.3 percent for Pakistan, but it had increased to 42.4 percent for the Republic of Korea[9]

While both generals had a vision for economic development, the base they established for this was very different. General Park Chung-hee is credited for successfully industrializing the Republic of Korea, establishing the base for its economic progress to high-income country status and joining the rich country club of the Organisation for Economic Co-operation and Development (OECD). General Ayub Khan willingly (to gain a political advantage) or inadvertently (due to weakness and incompetence) ushered in an era of crony capitalism that is still the bane of Pakistan's economy. Thus, while the Korean economic team ruthlessly demanded performance (quality exports) in exchange for limited time incentives, Pakistan was shielding industrialists from both external competition, via tariffs, and internal competition, via permits.[10] In 2010, garments topped the list of Pakistan's high-value exports,[11] and the cacophony of demands from industrialists for special privileges is still unceasing.[12]

Since, as indicated earlier, poor economic performance has been used as one of the main justifications for military intervention by all military regimes, we tested the hypothesis, using data from 1961 to 2009, that military regimes lead to better economic performance.[13] We found that military regimes do not result in superior economic growth, and nor did we find that poor economic performance results in military intervention.[14]

Olson (1993) makes an economic case for preferring democracy over autocracy on theoretical grounds. The empirical findings regarding the association of democracy and development, mostly using cross-country growth regressions, are mixed (Rivera-Batiz and Rivera-Batiz 2002, 143). Bowman (2002, 183–206) finds that militarization has a negative association with democracy, economic growth and equity for eighteen Latin American countries.

Khilji and Akhtar (1997) provide weak support of a negative association running from dictatorship to economic growth in Pakistan, but their empirical method was dated.[15] While we have reservations regarding growth regression on theoretical and measurement grounds, we nonetheless employed a standard growth equation, using an implicit production function and time series analysis, with GDP growth being explained by capital formation, labor and regime.[16] Our estimates suggest that a military regime accounts for 1.9 percent higher growth. However, although the result is statistically significant, we have little confidence in it because the equation we used to explain growth is very poor.[17]

We also compare the economic, social and human condition variables under the General Musharraf administration to that of the political administrations that preceded it (those of Prime Ministers Benazir Bhutto and Nawaz Sharif following the dictatorship of General Mohammad Zia-ul-Haq). The comparison is only suggestive, because much else, in terms of the internal and external conditions, could explain economic performance besides the competence of the economic management, civilian or military. Also, the impact of the policies of past governments can carry over to successive governments for at least a short time-period. Averaging over a number of years in each case, 10 for the political governments and 8 for the military governments, can partly resolve this problem. Ultimately, if the performance is not dramatically different, it would call into question the assumption of obvious superiority made by the military administrations.

As tables 1.1 to 1.4 show, there is reason to call into question this assumption since the comparative performance shows mixed results. Table 1.1 looks at fiscal and monetary discipline of the military administration relative to the political administrations that preceded it.

Table 1.1. Fiscal and monetary discipline and selected input indicators

	Political governments (1988–89/ 1998–99)	Military governments (1999–2000/2007–08)
Overall fiscal deficit as a % of GDP	7.00	4.40
Military expenditure as a % of GDP	5.82	3.20
Development expenditure as a % of GDP	5.02	3.42
Tax revenue as a % of GDP	13.55	10.70
Growth in money supply (M2)	15.12	15.60
Growth in capital formation	2.72	5.54
Public investment as a % of GDP	7.81	13.14
Private investment as a % of GDP	9.09	18.60
Foreign direct investment as a % of GDP*	0.85	1.53
Domestic savings as a % of GDP	10.24	16.12
Aid as a % of GNI*	2.21	1.71
Aid as a % of Federal Govt. expenditure*	10.71	10.59

Sources: Pakistan Economic Survey 2008–09, Statistical Appendix, pages 2–3. Information in rows marked with * are drawn from the World Bank, World Development Indicators, 2008. These time series only extend to 2007 and so the averages for the military government in these cases are over a shorter time period.

The most striking finding in table 1.1 is that military allocations as a percentage of GDP were almost twice as large under civilian administrations compared to the period of military rule.[18] It appears that when directly in charge, the military is forced to be more fiscally responsible. During nominally civilian regimes, it can bring pressure to bear behind the scenes. Looney (1989) cites evidence, using World Bank data for 31 countries, showing that this seems to be more broadly the case when comparing military to civilian regimes. However, while there might have been genuine cuts elsewhere, it appears that for Pakistan the cuts are a case of smoke and mirrors.

Military allocations are often camouflaged under the head of some other ministry. Also, *The New International* on 22 September 2010 reported that General Musharraf's administration removed military pensions from the military budget in 2001. They subsequently skyrocketed from Rs 26 billion in 2001 to Rs 76 billion in 2010 for the three million military retirees according to the Parliament Public Accounts Committee. This amounted to an average of Rs 24,000 per military retiree compared to Rs 3,600 per civilian retiree. Pakistan's military allocations in budget 2010–11 under a civilian regime represented a 16.5 percent increase relative to budget 2009–10. In addition to this direct allocation, the Defense Division also receives an allocation from the Public Development Sector Program for military projects.[19] The other surprising result is the much lower tax effort under the military government which once again calls into question its claims of superior economic management.

Beyond this, table 1.1 reveals that the military government subjected itself to the discipline of the IMF and its economic management team was very comfortable with this economic ideology.[20] While this shows up in better fiscal discipline (smaller fiscal deficit), the price was paid in terms of lower development expenditure as a percentage of GDP and in the form of low infrastructure development, as shown in table 1.2. Other macroeconomic indicators show better economic performance under the military administration with saving, capital formation and public and private investment as a percentage of GDP considerably higher under the military-led administration relative to the civilian governments. Table 1.2 explores output indicators corresponding to the input indicators in table 1.1.

Table 1.2 shows that the better input-indicators in terms of capital formation and private investment did not efficiently translate into outcome variables. The GDP growth rate of the military administration was only marginally higher than under the tenure of the civilian administrations. Also, exports as a percentage of GDP, a marker of the competitive quality of output, actually declined. However, the biggest failing was the lack of investment into the long-term future growth of the economy through building productive physical infrastructure. For example, the percentage growth in installed capacity for electricity, roads and telephones all declined multifold. The decline in growth of installed capacity of electricity from 110.8 percent to 10.5 percent could account for the electricity shortage during the last years

Table 1.2. Selected economic performance indicators (averages or growth rates)

	Political governments (1988–89/ 1998–99)	Military governments (1999–2000/2007–08)
GDP growth rate (%)	4.57	5.21
Manufacturing growth (%)	4.44	8.17
Agricultural growth (%)	4.61	3.16
Commodity producing sectors growth (%)	4.85	4.59
Services sector growth (%)	4.46	5.82
Inflation rate (GDP deflator)	10.24	7.43
Trade deficit as a % of GDP	4.87	3.58
Exports as a % of GDP	13.10	12.48
Imports as a % of GDP	17.90	16.03
Aggregate market capitalization of ordinary shares (% growth)	5.28	39.48
Electricity (% installed capacity growth)[#]	110.81	11.49
Roads (% growth)[#]	52.40	4.03
Telephones (% growth)	222.22	45.16
Electric power and distribution losses (%)[*]	22.85	25.03

Source: Pakistan Economic Survey 2008–09, Statistical Appendix, pages 2–7, 61. Information in rows marked with * is drawn from the World Bank, World Development Indicators, 2008. The average for military government is for the years from 1999 to 2003.
[#] represents growth for the political governments from 1989–90 to 1989–99.

of the Musharraf administration. Excessive load-shedding was endemic in 2010–12 in the country and sparked riots, and unfortunately it is likely to continue for a while.

However, the more serious failing of the military government was a reluctance to invest in improving the social and human condition of the population. Democratic administrations are answerable to the broader electorate and ignore such delivery at their electoral peril.

Table 1.3 shows that the commitment to education and health of the military administration was lower in terms of expenditure on these vital social sectors as a percentage of GDP. The crude outcome indicators also show poor performance of the military in most cases with schools and hospitals getting more crowded. Even worse was the comparative performance in terms of the human condition.

Table 1.3. Selected input and output indicators in the social sectors (averages)

	Political governments (1990–91/ 1998–99)	Military governments (1999–2000/2007–08)
Educational expenditure as a % of GDP	2.28	1.82
Health expenditure as a % of GDP	0.73	0.63
Population per hospital beds	1444.00	1486.60
Population per doctor	1810.00	1388.20
Student–institution ratio (primary)*	85.45	93.17
Student–teacher ratio (primary)*	32.82	37.22
Teacher–institution ratio (primary).	2.37	2.77

Source: Pakistan Economic Survey 2008–09, Statistical Appendix, pages 6–7, 85–87, 89. We constructed the education ratios from information available on students, teachers and institutions on pages 85–87.
* represents an average over 1992–93 to 1998–99 for the civilian government.

Unemployment increased and the real daily wage of unskilled workers decreased. It is not surprising then that the military administration's performance was much worse on various indicators of inequality and poverty. There was negative progress in reducing the Gini coefficient and much smaller progress in reducing poverty and the poverty gap.[21]

While inflation, which conditions real wages, was lower on average during the military administration period, it dramatically picked up in the last year of the Musharraf administration. The military government performed better on indicators of child and infant mortality rates and life expectancy, though not that of adult females. Overall however, based on economic, social and human condition variables, the assumption of overwhelming superiority of the management of the economy and society under military rule is called into question. Yet, despite this evidence, the military is likely to continue to assume that it is superior on all counts. This may have something to do with military training and the formation of the military mindset, which seems to avoid taking evidence into account.

Reforming the Military Mindset and Attaining Social Justice as a Pre-condition for Collective Action

Huntington (1959, chapter 3) uses the expression "The Military Mind" and provides associated references to earlier use. In the Pakistani context, Aziz (2008, 55) quotes Rahman (1973), a retired Lieutenant General, as writing: "Army mind – especially of those in appointments that mattered – had come

Table 1.4. Selected human condition indicators

	Political governments (1988–89/1989–99)	Military governments (1999–2000/2007–08)
Unemployment rate (% per annum)	5.19	6.96
Consumer price index (% growth)	10.39	6.24
Average deflated daily wage of unskilled labor	133.99#	144.79**
Average deflated daily wage of skilled labor	273.77#	217.72**
Percentage reduction in the Gini index	0 (1991–99)	–6.0 (1999–2005)
Percentage change in poverty gap at $1 per day (PPP)*	–79.3 (1991–99)	–33.0 (1999–2005)
Percentage change in poverty gap at $2 per day (PPP)	–47.7 (1991–99)	–17.4 (1999–2005)
Percentage change in headcount poverty ratio at $1 per day (PPP)	–55.4 (1991–99)	–20.7 (1999–2005)
Percentage change in headcount poverty ratio at $1 per day (PPP)	–23.9 (1991–99)	–11.7 (1999–2005)
Percentage reduction in IMR (per 1000)	8.9 (1990–2000)	9.7 (2000–05)
Percentage reduction in <5 mortality rate (per 1000)	9.8 (1990–99)	14.7 (2000–07)
Percentage increase in female life expectancy at birth	3.6 (1990–99)	8.0 (2000–05)
Percentage increase in male life expectancy at birth	1.7 (1990–99)	3.5 (2000–05)
Reduction in adult female mortality rate (per 1000)	25.6 (1990–99)	12.6 (2000–07)
Reduction in adult male mortality rate (per 1000)	10.6 (1990–99)	11.6 (2000–07)

Source: Pakistan Economic Survey 2008–09, Statistical Appendix, pages 2–3, 6–7. We computed the average deflated daily wages using the general price index, Government of Pakistan, Statistical Appendix 2006, page 51. Nominal wages for skilled and unskilled labor were available from the same source, page 101. A straight average of wages for skilled and unskilled labor across the federal and provincial capital cities was used. The wage series is for the calendar years while the price index is for the fiscal years, so the price indices for two overlapping years (1990–91 and 1991–92) were averaged to make it consistent for deflating the fiscal-year wage series (1991). All data after the first four variables are drawn from the World Bank's World Development Indicators. The time periods for these variables are indicated in the parentheses after the values because they differ by variable.
represents an average over 1988–98. ** represents an average over 1999–2008. PPP is purchasing power parity. IMR is infant mortality rate.

to accept and expect that [the] Army as a whole could take on any and every problem of the State." We use the term mindset as the reference is to attitudes, a subset of the broader concept.

This sense of superiority has little justification. While the section above shows a very poor record in terms of interventions in the economy, civil society or in managing the economy and society as a whole, the Pakistani military's war record has also been abysmal. In addition, it has sought military solutions for political problems and this has been equally disastrous; Bangladesh and Balochistan are cases in point. General Musharraf's remark, "they won't know what hit them," when referring to a struggle for social justice in Balochistan, suggests a mindset that is too easily willing to view fellow citizens as enemies. The 2009 campaigns in Swat and South Waziristan redeemed the military in some civilian eyes, but most savvy political observers view the military as now confronting problems it created by recruiting and using religious fundamentalists for foreign policy objectives.

The military systematically creates a binary world view opposing the superior "us" to "them." The latter are the civilians who simply are not good enough. Even a soldier dismissively waves off any civilian, no matter how distinguished, who accidently drives towards one of the many barriers put up in the heart of cities to block the roads leading to military cantonments.

Underlying the drive to ensure the welfare of retired military officials is the arrogant assumption that their future welfare is more important than those of their fellow citizens. Thus, they have taken it in to their hands, by drawing on a disproportionate amount of state resources, to ensure that military personnel, particularly the senior officer corps, are well taken care of when they retire.

In this disproportionate drawing of resources, the military represents a constraint on the economy and the wellbeing of the rest of society. In so far as its competition with the private sector is not based on a level playing-field, it crowds out private sector activity. In any case, as argued above, such activity is beyond the mandate and competence of the military.[22]

When queried on the justification for their special entitlements and privileges, military officers often respond that they are the ones taking the bullets. First, a military occupation is a choice. Second, no citizen would begrudge military personnel who demonstrated bravery in the line of fire or those who made the ultimate sacrifice. But this does not justify extending asymmetrical privileges to the whole institution rising by rank. Such practices create social resentment as we document later in the book.

We noted above that sustained economic take-off in Pakistan is unlikely to be based on exceptional administrative and managerial capacity, and it never exclusively is. It is, at the moment, also unlikely to draw strength from broad ranging national identification with a common economic development project. For the latter, the high handedness and disproportionate claim of resources by the military, the corruption of the political elites and the civil bureaucracy, the denial of rights to small provinces and the oppression of religious and ethnic minorities would have to end. In other words, national identification with a common project would require the implementation and perception of social justice.

While the economic development project does not wait for initial conditions to be satisfied, such as social justice, the latter is needed for a solid base. Most countries charge headlong into the economic development project and the fortunate ones find social justice, administrative and managerial capacity, and accountability to be endogenous to the process. In such cases, a virtuous circle is created and a take-off assured. The rest, like Pakistan, huddle together at the bottom of the charts of human and economic development.

In exploring the role of the military in Pakistan's agrarian society and economy in chapters 4 to 7 of this book, the most important economic development issue we confronted in the field was that of the commons. In all societies, the commons (public land) belong to current and future generations. In democratic societies, enlightened elected representatives act on behalf of not only current but also future generations (for example, the Norwegian oil-earnings-based sovereign wealth fund). In Pakistan, the military summarily demands access to the commons for allocations to soldiers, non-commissioned officers (NCOs), junior commissioned officers (JCOs), and junior and particular senior military officers in both cities and rural areas. These demands are ongoing, as indicated in chapter 5, and they undermine the perception of social justice and identification with a common economic development project. In our view, an important constraint for the building of a consensus for effective national collective action, and hence a take-off, is the perception of social injustice and the military has much to do with this.

Conclusion

Successive military coups in Pakistan have been justified in terms of economic incompetence and corruption of political administrations. We provide evidence in this chapter that the militarization of economic life is inefficient and crowds out private sector activity. We also demonstrate that there is no evidence to support the claim that military administrations are more competent in managing the economy, or indeed less corrupt. There is evidence to suggest that they may invest less in social and physical infrastructure and that their term in office coincides with increased poverty and inequality and a more generalized deterioration of the human condition. This is as one might expect, since they are not answerable to a political constituency.

To restore the military to its primary function of defense requires rolling back the military's economic autonomy based on equitable treatment of military and non-military bureaucracies based on the constraints imposed by the economy. There is also a need for a durable peace with India based on some kind of just compromise and resolution of the Kashmir issue that addresses the aspirations of the Kashmiri people. This conflict makes it easy for the military to draw disproportionate allocations for weapons systems and its bloated welfare needs relative to the rest of society.

The previous (2008–2013) chief of army staff, General Kayani, was viewed as believing in a separation of military and political functions. However, such claims have been made in the past. But then, as now, the separation was not institutionalized – it depended on an individual.[23] An important mechanism for the institutionalization of elected government is to change the economic power balance by rolling back the military's economic dominance.

Thus, as important as the military's separation from politics is the accompanying separation of the military from the economy. As argued above, there is evidence that the militarization of economic life is inefficient and crowds out private sector activity. All public officials need to be equitably assured a reasonable retirement based on economic constraints, but large, unwieldy and inefficient foundation-run conglomerates are not the way to do this. Public policy could start with dismantling operations that cannot survive in a transparent budgeting environment without undue market power, cross-subsidies within the military budget or state subsidies.

The problem of economic development, a national project, can be thought of in terms of identifying what is most likely to galvanize the populations to accept short-term sacrifices and do the hard work.[24] In China's case, we identified managerial and administrative capacity and patriotism as central. Patriotism does not simply emerge with crude attempts at persuasion in the syllabi and the media. In Pakistan's case, it is only likely to emerge in a deep sense once the perception is created that social justice is being administered by rolling back the military's disproportionate privileges. It is also likely in principle that there would be more success in addressing ethnic, sectarian and class divides that undermine national cohesion if the military was not such a heavy political and financial burden on the nation. In the rest of the book we explore the role of the military in Punjab's (Pakistan's most populated province) agrarian society and economy as a case study on how the perception of social justice is undermined and the general population socially alienated and unlikely to engage in effective national collective action.

Notes

1 Thanks to Daniel Altschuler, Daniel Barbezat and James Boyce for comments and suggestions on this chapter. This chapter is an extended version of a paper written for a Feschrift to honor Tom Weisskopf at the University of Massachusetts in October 2011 and published in: R. Pollin and Wicks-Lim, J. 2013. *Capitalism on Trial: Explorations in the Tradition of Thomas E. Weisskopf.* Northampton: Edward Elgar.

2 While the reference throughout this book is to the military, the army, with about 58 percent of the total active duty personnel, is predominant in power and influence.

3 The other provinces are Balochistan, Sindh and Khyber-Phukunkhwa. The major ethnic groups in the country by population are Punjabis (44.1%), Pathans or Pushtuns (15.42%), Sindhis (14.10%), Seraikis (10.53%, part of Punjab Province), Muhajir (7.57%, originally Urdu speaking refugees that mainly settled in Karachi, Sindh during partition) and Balochis (3.57%). The numbers are dated since the latest Population Census was conducted in 1998, and the 2008 Population Census results had not been released at the time of writing. Appendix 3.4 shows provincial demarcations.

4 An example of a vicious circle would be ethnic and social conflicts leading to low investment, low growth, a lack of resources and more ethnic and social conflict.

5 More complex societies continue to face more complex managerial challenges (e.g. financial collapses) and so the process of learning and moving on and facing new challenges is never ending.

6 This contrasts with Cuba which has stuck with its socialist philosophy and ranks as a high human development nation with an index of 0.863 in 2007 (UNDP 2009, 167–68). The Gini is a measure of social inequality with complete social equality at 0 and maximum inequality at 1. Data are taken from various issues of the World Bank *World Development Reports.*

7 See for example http://www.thedailystar.net/newDesign/news-details.php?nid=166390.

8 This arrogance was carried to an extreme degree when military officers were appointed as civilian watchdogs. This created resentment and, to add insult to injury, the officers knew little about what they were supervising. This practice of inducting military personnel into civilian life was institutionalized by General Zia who set a quota of 10 percent of civilian jobs in civilian administration for military personal (Aziz 2008, 71).

9 Commons.wikimedia.org/…/File:Per_capita_GDP_of_South_Asian_economies_ &_ Skorea_ (1950–95).

10 Refer to Wade (2004) for a review of Korean economic development strategy and Papanek (1967) for Pakistan's economic development strategy at an equivalent time period. Korea's experience shows that a national project can be autocratically induced. While this is superior to a predatory dictatorial regime, we view achieving an economic take-off with public identification and participation in a common national project as superior.

11 In July to April of 2009–10, at 53 percent of total exports, textiles topped the list of Pakistan's exports (Government of Pakistan 2010, 89) while in 2010 Korea was edging out Japan in automobile exports to the US market.

12 In 2010, there was a virtual textile war. The spinning subsector was demanding cheap cotton, the weaving subsector cheap yarn, and the garment subsector cheap fabric. Each was demanding this at the expense of the other subsectors earlier in the value chain and the imposition of export restrictions was the common demand.

13 Data were drawn from the World Bank's on line World Development Indicators.

14 Our tests only explored a limited form of causality referred to in the time series econometric literature as Granger causality. For a basic treatment of the subject, refer to Gujarati (1995, 620–23).

15 They do not use co-integration.

16 The Johansen co-integration test suggested our growth equation was co-integrated at the 5 percent level.

17 The R bar square is 13 percent which is very low, especially for a time series regression. Also, the result is clearly not robust since both investment and labor are statistically insignificant in explaining economic growth. Most important, we only found investment data between 1980 and 2008, and hence missed about half the relevant economic history.

18 In 2008, Pakistan Armed Forces were almost three times larger as a percentage of the labor force (1.65) than the Indian Armed forces (0.57) See World Bank World Development Indicators at http://databank.worldbank.org/ddp/home. do?Step=12&id=4&CNO=2.

19 These are nontrivial allocations that for 2010–2011 amounted to 5.86 percent of the total Public Sector Development Program. See: http://app.com.pk/en_/index. php?option=com_cont ent&task=view&id=105227&Itemid=174. Thanks are due to Saba Gul Khattak for suggesting this inquiry.

20 Civilian governments, including the current one (2013–), have also been subject to the discipline of the IMF. However, in the past, there have been many recriminations on the part of these financial institutions about violations of conditionality while the military government of General Musharraf was given high marks in this regard. See Khan (2007).

21 The numbers understate the performance of the political governments or overstate the performance of the military government in terms of the reduction of the poverty gaps. Since the gap had already been reduced by the political governments, a given percentage reduction by the military government means a smaller absolute reduction since the base is smaller. Thanks are due to Christopher Kingsley for pointing this out.

22 The Pakistan military has often won kudos from international organizations for its administrative and organizational ability in dealing with disasters such as with floods and the 2006 earthquake in Pakistan administered Kashmir or the 2010 floods that devastated virtually the whole country. Given that the military's constitutionally mandated role is defense, it should train civil authorities to develop their disaster mitigation, preparedness and management abilities and then withdraw once this is done and the appropriate resource reallocation has taken place.

23 Generals Asif Nawaz and Abdul Waheed Kakar were chiefs of army staff in 1991–93 and 1993–96 respectively and were cases in point in that they were both praised by politicians as thoroughly professional soldiers who kept the army out of politics.

24 Chang (2006) points out that even when South Korea became a successful auto-producing country, it continued for a while to have lower per-capita consumption of cars than in low income countries of Sub-Saharan Africa and South Asia with a much lower per-capita GDP.

References

Acemoglu, D. and J. A. Robinson. 2006. *Economic Origins of Dictatorship and Democracy.* Cambridge: Cambridge University Press.

Aziz, M. 2008. *Military Control in Pakistan: The Parallel State.* London: Routledge.

Bhave, A. and C. Kingston. 2010. "Military Coups and the Consequences of Durable de facto Power: The Case of Pakistan." *Economics of Governance* 11 (1), 51–76.

Bowman, K. S. 2002, *Militarization, Democracy, and Development*. University Park: Pennsylvania State University Press.

Cloughley, B. 2008. *War, Coups, & Terror: Pakistan's Army in Years of Turmoil*. New York: Skyhorse Publishing.

Chang, H.-J. 2010. "Hamlet without the Prince of Denmark: How Development Has Disappeared from Today's 'Development' Discourse." *Towards New Developmentalism: Market as Means rather than Master*. New York: Routledge.

Chang, H.-J. 2006. *The East Asian Development Experience: The Miracle, the Crisis and the Future*. London: Zed Books.

Cohen, S. P. 1994. *The Pakistan Army*. Karachi: Oxford University Press.

Dixit, A. 2007. "Evaluating Recipes for Development Success." *The World Bank Research Observer* 22 (2), 131–57.

Dobell, G. 2003. "Australia and Indonesia's Military Mafia." *Agenda* 10 (1), 3–12.

Firat, D. 2005. "Militarization of the Market and Rent-Seeking Coalitions in Turkey." *Development and Change* 34 (4), 667–90.

Gallagher, K. P. and M. Shafaeddin. 2010. "Governing Reform and Industrial Development in China and India." In *Towards New Developmentalism: Market as Means rather than Master*. New York: Routledge.

Government of Pakistan. 2010. *Pakistan Economic Survey 2009–2010*. Islamabad: Government of Pakistan.

Gujarati, D. M. 1995. *Basic Econometrics*, Third Edition. New York: McGraw Hill.

Hausmann, R., B. Klinger and R. Wagner. 2008. "Doing Growth Diagnostics in Practice: A 'Mindbook.'" *Center for International Development Working Paper No. 177*. Cambridge, MA: Harvard University Press.

Huntington, S. P. 1959. *The Soldier and the State: The Theory and Politics of Civil-Military Relations*. Cambridge: Belknap Press of Harvard University Press.

Khan, S. R. 2007. "Pakistan's Economy since 1999: Has There Been Real Progress?" *South Asia Economic Journal* 8 (1), 317–34.

Khilji, N. M. and Akhtar, M. 1997. "Military Expenditure and Economic Growth in Pakistan." *Pakistan Development Review* 36 (4), 791–806.

LaFraniere, S. "Fighting Trend, China Is Luring Scientists Home." *New York Times*, 6 January 2010.

Looney, R. E. 1989. "The Economic Impact of Rent Seeking and Military Expenditures: A Comparision of Third World Military and Civilian Regimes." *American Journal of Economics and Sociology* 48 (1), 11–29.

Olson, M. 1993, "Dictatorship, Democracy and Development." *The American Political Science Review* 87 (3), 567–576.

Papanek, G. F. 1967. *Pakistan's Development: Social Goals and Private Incentives*. Cambridge, MA: Harvard University Press.

Rahman, M. A. 1973. *Leadership: Senior Commanders*. Lahore: Ferozsons.

Rivera-Batiz, F. L. and L. A. Rivera-Batiz. 2002. "Democracy, Participation and Development." *Review of Development Economics* 6 (2), 135–50.

Rodrik, D. 2010. "Diagnostics before Prescription." *Journal of Economic Perspectives* 24 (3), 33–44.

Rostow, W. 1960. *The Stages of Economic Growth: A Non-Communist Manifesto*. Cambridge: Cambridge University Press.

Siddiqa, A. 2007. *Military Inc.: Inside Pakistan's Military Economy*. Karachi: Oxford University Press.

Tse-tung, M. 1968. *Four Essays in Philosophy*. Beijing: Foreign Language Press.

UNDP. 2009. *Human Development Report 2009*. New York: UNDP.

Wade, R. H. 2004. *Governing the Market: Economic Theory and the Role of Government in East Asian Industrialization*. Princeton: Princeton University Press.

World Bank. 2010. *World Development Report 2010*. Washington DC: World Bank.

Zweig, D. 2006. "Competing for Talent: China's Strategies to Reverse the Brain Drain." *International Labour Review* 145 (1–2), 65–89.

Chapter Two

PUNJAB'S STATE–SOCIETY CONSENSUS ON THE MILITARY'S DOMINANCE AND ECONOMIC ROLE

Introduction

While the Pakistani military's economic empire has unquestionably been built on the back of the institution's coercive power, one of the central premises of this book is that the military's political and economic preeminence has been sustained by a critical mass of support from within Punjabi society. In this chapter we briefly explore the unique colonial social contract forged in what is today's Pakistani Punjab and discuss the various factors that reinforced this social contract in the postcolonial period. Subsequently, we argue that the military's insatiable appetite to expand its economic empire is unveiling contradictions within Punjabi society that were previously latent. There are signs that the state–society consensus – both cause and consequence of the military's dominance and economic role – has started to break down. Finally, we draw on our historical overview to discuss state theory in Pakistan to explore the military's power as a function of both its coercive power and consent generated from below.

Punjabi State–Society Relations in the Colonial Period

Punjab is, in every sense, Pakistan's heartland. It is the country's most populous, economically rich and politically influential province. It is also predominantly the home of the Pakistani military. The majority of the military's recruits hail from the Punjab, while cantonments are spread out across the length and breadth of the province.[1] Including paramilitary forces and reserves, the Pakistani military was about 1.4 million strong in 2010, which means that substantial economic and political benefits are garnered by a sizeable proportion of Punjab's labor force through its affiliation with the military, both direct and indirect.[2] Only a century ago, however, Punjab's demographic, economic and political landscapes were very different.

While its eastern regions were better populated, what is today Pakistani Punjab featured substantial nomadic populations and scattered settled areas. The flow of Punjab's five rivers dictated agrarian settlement and it was not until the British undertook their epic canal irrigation revolution that the foundations of modern Punjabi society were laid.

As has been ably documented by Ali (1988) and others in his wake, the design and construction of a network of perennial irrigation canals in the interfluves between Punjab's five rivers heralded the creation of a unique 'hydraulic society' that accorded to Punjab a privileged position in the political and economic hierarchy of the Raj.[3] The so-called canal colonies were the epitome of colonial benevolence – in engineering a social order virtually from scratch, the British hoped to ensure a permanent and mutual relationship between the state and its subjects that could demonstrate to all Indians the benefits of supporting the colonial power.

All of the eight major canal colonies built by the British starting from 1885 featured a rhetorical and practical emphasis on the individual peasant proprietor. The British firmly believed that the sparse local populations were incapable of effectively colonizing the irrigated lands and thereby inmigrated peasants of the sturdy type from east Punjab. The majority of grantees in all canal colonies were peasants who were allocated two squares (1 square equals 25 acres) of land each. In short, the so-called new society that came into being under late colonial rule – and what was to become the most populous and economically developed region of Pakistan – owed its very existence to the state.

There were – and are, of course – significant differences even within the canal colony areas between newly settled *chaks* (villages) and older villages and towns that had developed along the river banks prior to the British period.[1] However, our contention is that the political and economic benefits of British paternalism in the canal colony areas were more or less shared across this divide. More substantive social, political and economic differences existed between the canal colony regions and the arid Potohar plateau in northwestern Punjab that supplied the majority of the army's recruits. In much the same way as the development of perennial irrigation canals served a distinct colonial ordering objective, the underdevelopment of the Potohar plateau facilitated a permanent supply of army men, and an attendant reinforcement of cultural essentialism constructed around the myth of the martial castes.[5] The link between the underdevelopment of Potohar and the development in the canal colonies was made through the systematic issuing of land grants in the canal colonies to retired military personnel in recognition of their services to the Raj. As such then, the peasant-soldier became the quintessential support base of colonial rule in the Punjab.

In the older southern and western districts of the province, the British relied more on the prototypical landed elite that has been identified so closely with colonial rule in India. As a general rule, the Siraiki-speaking areas remained relatively isolated from the militarized regions of Punjab and therefore boasted distinct political, economic and cultural structures. Indeed, large parts of the Siraiki belt were encapsulated in very different administrative and political arrangements, including the princely state of Bahawalpur. To some extent, these historical-structural differences explain the more confrontational political idiom that exists in the Siraiki belt in the contemporary period against both Punjabi dominance and the military's institutional power.[6]

In so far as the landowning core of British Punjab was constituted by a curious mix of established landed aristocrats, rich farmers and the middle peasantry, the state took care to keep all three class fractions co-opted within official patronage networks. The landed elite had preferential access to political and economic resources at the national and provincial levels; the rich farmers were in control of the formal institutional networks at the local level, while even the middle peasantry was kept satiated by a relatively fluid legal structure that emphasized certain caste and kinship distinctions (Javid 2011).

Tan (2005) has shown that the colonial social order in Punjab featured a set of political institutions that brought all privileged social forces under a common umbrella. Crucially, military personnel were intricately involved in the business of administration and also given suffrage, whereas the majority of Punjabis, specifically those who did not own land, were not. A unique form of government was institutionalized, popularly known as the Punjab school of administration, in which authoritarian tendencies were not only present but were in fact encouraged (Tan 2005, 219).[7] The electoral regime created and refined by the British from 1919 onwards reinforced the unique civil-military regime, based as it was on a very deeply ingrained principle of distribution of patronage and heavily skewed towards rural-military interests.[8]

A significant segment of Punjabi society did not benefit unambiguously from the colonial social contract. So-called nonagriculturalists, and particularly landless menials, were neither entitled to land grants nor considered worthy of being designated warriors. However, the division between winners and losers of the colonial project was less pronounced in the canal colony areas than in other parts of India where social engineering initiatives were much less ambitious. Indeed, in some canal colony districts, the British even accepted the rights of so-called *janglis* (literally barbarians of the forest) to a share of land.[9] Nevertheless, the landless underclass of Punjabis remained, as have latent tensions between them, in the British nomenclature, agriculturalists and nonagriculturalists.[10]

In sum, the British had fashioned a settler-indigenous society in Punjab that was intricately co-opted into the patronage networks of the state. It was thus that the dominant political idiom in the province was that of 'agriculturalists' operating under the guise of the Punjab Unionist Party. While the Muslim League did eventually secure a (tenuous) support base in some parts of the province in the heady last couple of years leading up to the British departure, the huge upheavals that took place in and around the transfer of power reinforced rather than undermined the historical consensus between a cross-section of Punjabi society and the postcolonial state.

Punjabi State–Society Relations in the Postcolonial Period: The Defense Imperative

The new state was formed under tumultuous circumstances that provided an opportunity for the bureaucracy, military and propertied classes of West Pakistan to emphasize the imperative of national security at the cost of promoting the fledgling political process. This imperative was simply not questioned by mainstream political forces or for that matter within the wider society in which avenues for dissenting political opinion were extremely limited (Rizvi 2003, 76).[11] The 'garrison state' model in which civil and military power were considered two sides of the same coin was seamlessly interwoven into the worldview of the administrators of the new state.[12]

In the early years, the military garnered a disproportionate share of public resources; it accounted for 70 percent of the budget expenditure in the first year of Pakistan's formation (Siddiqi 1996, 70). Over time, the budget allocation to the military has decreased. Yet, as Cheema (2003, 44) notes: "Many defense items are camouflaged and are listed under some other ministry's budgetary allocation. These are known as hidden allocations – resources allocated to the non-defense sector but whose outcome forms a significant part of the overall defense activity."[13]

As pointed out in chapter 1, the defense budget is not the only form of a disproportionate drawing of resources by the military. Institutionalized claims on welfare for its personnel are enormous and far in excess of what the state can afford. These claims have resulted in the establishment of a business, finance and commercial empire and the transfer to military personnel of disproportionate shares of the commons in the form of residential and agricultural state land. The colonial policy of allotting land on the border to senior (and increasingly junior) military men continued with the inception of the new state, with the threat from India invoked as one particular justification.

This policy of issuing land allotments meant that military personnel enjoyed a symbiotic relationship with migrants who had been given ownership of evacuated lands in the same regions. More generally, nationalist sentiment, and the anti-India consciousness in particular, was concentrated primarily amongst the migrant communities of Punjab and urban Sindh. Scholars have documented the immensely influential role of migrants in the new state and have pointed out that their political weight and economic power was disproportionate to their actual size in the population (Waseem 2004). Given the deep psychological impacts of partition violence that the migrants had witnessed first hand, it was not surprising that the ideology of national security found a home in Punjab (Waseem 1999).[11]

Our fieldwork for this book indicated latent tensions between land allottees (whether military personnel or migrants) and local communities have persisted.[15] Alavi (1982, 26) noted that the peculiar nature of the evacuee land policy made for a "reverse land reform" in the early 1950s whereby smallholders were actually deprived of their lands and overall distribution of productive assets in rural Punjab became more inegalitarian. To some extent these latent tensions – which as we have noted existed between agriculturalists and nonagriculturalists, even in the British period – took the form of political protest at particular periods in the first couple of decades after Pakistan's creation; the most prominent example in this regard was the popular movement in Punjab in the late 1960s which paved the way to power for the Pakistan People's Party (PPP). However, we concur with scholars who have noted that even when Prime Minister Zulfiqar Ali Bhutto's populism established substantial roots in Punjab, anti-India nationalism and a militaristic ideology more generally remained very widespread amongst a broad cross-section of Punjabi society.[16]

Dewey (1991) points to a symbiotic link between "a militaristic ideology" that has deep historical roots in rural Punjab and the military-dominated political (and economic) order. We agree that purely functional political and economic explanations for the military's dominance (and its relative popularity) in the Punjab must be supplemented by an understanding of norms and values in Punjabi culture that have facilitated militarism. The logical end of this argument is, however, too similar to the orientalist interpretation of Punjabis being bearers of an unchanging martial tradition and not one we are at all comfortable with. Yet, the history of Punjab since at least the Sikh empire of Ranjit Singh suggests that the military profession has indeed been considered very honorable, at least in the Potohar and canal colony regions.

The Eroding State–Society Consensus: The Birth of a New Punjab?

Our argument that the consent generated within Punjab for the military's overarching role in the economic and political spheres is now starting to fracture reflects changing norms and values that are coeval with a rapidly modernizing society. The secondary and tertiary sectors of Punjab's agrarian economy have developed dramatically since 1947, urbanization has proceeded apace, and at least some Punjabis have become aware of the fact that the military's monopoly over political and economic resources directly impinges on their own economic and social wellbeing.

In the first few years after the inception of the state, the latent tensions between propertied and nonpropertied classes in general and the military and disenfranchised segments of society in particular were kept in check by the state's reinforcement of a militarist ideology. As parliamentary government failed to take root in the first decade of the country's existence (see next section), with different factions competing to win favor with a powerful civil bureaucracy, the military – and importantly a significant section of the intelligentsia – propagated the myth that it offered stability and direction and greater efficiency in comparison to politicians. In chapter 1, we demonstrated that the military has been found wanting in government, its management of the economy, economic activities and even defense. Nonetheless, during fieldwork, we observed that the project of demeaning politicians has been vastly successful. Cynicism and mistrust about the intent and performance of politicians is rife, although subordinate classes in rural areas are far less contemptuous about the political class than the educated classes who are not compelled to engage regularly with the *thana* (police station), *katcheri* (court) and other institutions of the state.

The military's aura was built up through "heroic" episodes of assistance to civilian authority in the wake of natural and man-made disasters (Rizvi 2000, 7–8).[17] As – if not more – important has been the management of public disturbances such as the Ahmadi riots of 1953, when the first martial law in the independent country's history was imposed. By taking responsibility for the restoration of the public peace, the military very deliberately cultivated an image for itself as the ultimate guardian of the state.

The former director general of Inter-Services Public Relations (ISPR) under General Mohammad Ayub Khan, Brigadier A. R. Siddiqui, writes that the military has always preferred to maintain a distance from the wider society, which has been crucial to its image as "guardian of the state." This so-called Sher Ali formula has emphasized the demeaning of politicians who come into contact with the mass of people and whose self-aggrandizement and immaturity have exposed them to consistent public censure.[18] This staying above the fray in classic colonial tradition is a grand concept, but the military has been badly sullied by its performance during many bouts of extra-constitutional rule, and more generally, as we argue, by its increasingly voracious resource-grabbing antics.

The first of such obvious public relations disasters for the military came in the late 1960s with General Mohammad Ayub Khan's fall from grace. Repressive labor legislation and the Green Revolution, which the general had championed in the early years of his rule, set the stage for the social and political upheaval that culminated in his political demise. As urban inequality and landlessness (due to the introduction of labor-saving technologies) grew, political radicalism both amongst the fledgling industrial working class and the peasantry spread, and the latent tensions that we have highlighted above took the form of overt social conflict[19]. Importantly, Alavi (1983) has noted that among the major beneficiaries of the Green Revolution were retired civil and military personnel who either already possessed or were allotted fertile irrigated lands in the Punjab and Sindh and had the requisite capital to invest in the new technologies.

The political idiom in Punjab in the late 1960s and early 1970s did not pose land-grabbing military personnel as the immediate adversary of landless Punjabis (or Pakistanis for that matter), and so the military as an institution escaped without major censure even while other landlords, industrialists and bureaucrats were depicted as class enemies of the people. This movement propelled Zulfiqar Ali Bhutto to the post of president (1971–73) and then prime minister (1973–77), following an interregnum under General Agha Mohammad Yahya Khan (1969–71) who presided over a disastrous civil war in East Pakistan (now Bangladesh).

Following the dismemberment of the country in December 1971, the public myth of the military's omnipotence was crushed. This was reflected in scathing attacks on military professionalism in major newspapers; editorials lamented that the military's humiliating surrender in East Pakistan was a direct outcome of the military's negligence of its professional duties during its prolonged time in power (Shafqat 1997, 166). Accordingly, the Bhutto regime was presented with an unprecedented opportunity to relegate the military to a position of subservience to civilian authority.

As much as any other regime in Pakistan's history, the PPP government reasserted the national security paradigm and, particularly, the anti-India imperative; providing a golden opportunity for the military to reemerge as a major actor in a power-sharing arrangement. Defense expenditures increased markedly under the PPP government, while it also initiated the nuclear program, which has subsequently become a major pillar of the national security state.[20]

Bhutto also employed the military liberally to quell internal dissent against industrial labor in Karachi and urban centers in Punjab, thereby also rehabilitating its complementary law and order function. Perhaps most crucially, the military was called in to crush a nationalist movement in Balochistan in

1973, a mere 18 months after the eastern wing of the country had been lost because of the western wing's unwillingness to fashion an equitable power-sharing arrangement. Historically, the military's image as guardian of the state has been synonymous with the use of force against nationalist movements for autonomy (Alavi 1987, 106–7). The Balochistan episode reignited the flames of chauvinism in the Punjab against oppressed nationalities and was central to the restoration of the Punjabi-dominated military's prestige.

Under General Mohammad Zia-ul-Haq (1977–1988), the military confirmed its rehabilitation in the Punjabi public's eye. This rehabilitation in part reflects the fact that the wider social and economic transformation that followed the Green Revolution led to a consolidation of Punjab's – and therefore Punjabis' – privileged position within Pakistan. Industrialization and its multiplier effects meant that, to a greater extent than any other province, working-class Punjabis had some avenues for social mobility.[21] In the late 1970s, thousands of Punjabis from mostly rural backgrounds migrated to the Gulf and the remittance incomes that subsequently accrued to these households also had a major stabilizing effect on society (Addleton 1992).

Indeed, Punjab has changed in not insignificant ways due to the rise of a middle class in the postcolonial period, and particularly since the 1970s. A quite vibrant middle class has existed in the province from the colonial period, both in the form of commercial elements enmeshed in the secondary and tertiary sectors of the agrarian economy and the salaried professionals who were so deeply involved in the independence movement. Crucially, of course, before 1947 a majority of the commercial segments of this middle class was non-Muslim; partition thus enfranchised many (Muslim) landed influentials in Punjab doubly, in so far as they took over much of the business left behind by non-Muslim migrants (Alavi 1990, 29–30).

However, beyond the landed classes' reinvention of itself is a story of substantial upward mobility from within relatively less affluent segments of Punjabi society. With the monies generated from migrations (to urban centers or outside the country), a large number of households in north and central Punjab – the Siraiki belt less so – has invested in small-scale enterprise in sectors as diverse as transport, agricultural machinery and seed dealing. In short, while a significant proportion of Punjab's historically deprived classes have remained on the margins, urbanization has proffered opportunities to an emergent middle class to qualitatively alter its accumulation and consumption patterns.[22]

Unfortunately, the evidence seems to suggest that these emergent middle classes have no necessary proclivity towards democracy, having secured much of their own upward mobility by learning the ropes of the military-dominated authoritarian socio-political order that has remained intact in some shape or another since the colonial period. Indeed, the middle classes have arguably evinced a great deal of cynicism towards politics that impedes the emergence of a broad consensus across society forcing the military into retreat (Zaidi 2005).

Yet there is also a countervailing trend. Since 2007, when the Musharraf dictatorship started to collapse, segments of the middle classes have been more vociferously articulating overt criticism of the military's dominance and the ideology of the state, which the military purports to defend. The ethnic divide, even within the middle class, appears to map historical alignments – the non-Punjabi middle classes are more likely to dissent, whereas their Punjabi counterparts remain more co-opted into the networks of political and economic patronage cultivated by the military and its hangers-on.

Notwithstanding historical continuities, the opening up of spaces for dissent within Punjab should induce at least a segment of the middle classes to stand with the subordinate classes who remain the primary victims of the military's excesses. More generally, one of the most important qualitative changes that has taken place in Punjabi society over the past three decades pertains to how ordinary Punjabis relate to the militarist ideology that has propped up the state-society consensus in the province. While the patriarchal notion of valor remains a defining feature in Punjabi culture, many things have changed. First, the military profession is no longer the only stable and/or prestigious life choice available to working-age males in the traditional recruiting grounds. Second, the military's land grabbing in recent years has become ever more blatant – as rent (in cash rather than in kind) tenure arrangements become more commonplace – and military personnel have become more and more prominent as absentee landlords. As we document in chapters 4 and 5, whether in the form of border allotments that began under General Mohammad Ayub Khan or in non-border areas within districts such as Okara and Muzaffargarh, military land grabbing has become ever more rapacious, in contradistinction to the aspired to 'above the fray' Sher Ali formula.

For the best part of Pakistan's existence, the military's role as guardian of the state has been deeply internalized in the Punjab. In some cases, land grabbing has taken place through pure coercion of a helpless population that is fearful of being branded anti-Pakistan. More generally the military has generated consent for these practices by sharing some of the spoils with other agriculturalists, and indeed with a wider cross section of society that can be broadly termed the emergent middle classes. However, as time has progressed, more and more ordinary civilian populations have come into contact with military men and been exposed to economic terror, which typically takes place under the guise of the greater national interest. Our research shows the elements of fear, co-option and genuine consent that defined the attitudes of ordinary Punjabis towards the military's burgeoning economic empire in the past have started to unravel in the face of the growing evidence that the military is not in fact guardian of the state, but instead guardian of its own interests.

Working-class Punjabis remain better off as a general rule than working Sindhis, Baloch, Pashtun, Siraikis or Kashmiris.[23] As we have asserted above, Punjab has remained the economic heartland of the country, and the benefits of growth – however skewed – have trickled down to even working-class Punjabis to a much greater extent than elsewhere in the country. Yet, growing landlessness and economic hardship in the era of neoliberal adjustment is taking its toll on working-class Punjabis and, their relative affluence notwithstanding, this too is leading to intensified resentment towards the military and its land grabbing. We turn now to state theory to put into context this short historical brief.

The Military and the State in Pakistan

There has been no consolidated attempt to theorize the Pakistani state since the pioneering work of Hamza Alavi.[24] The acclaimed work of Ayesha Siddiqa – upon which this book builds – focuses more on the empirics of the military corporate empire and addresses theoretical concerns only fleetingly. We too are engaging with the (sparse) theoretical debate very briefly here – and specifically with the objective of establishing that it is only possible to understand the structure of power in Pakistan if attention is paid to questions of legitimation as much as the relationships between dominant institutional and class interests.

For our purposes, Alavi's most important contributions are his concepts of mediation and relative autonomy. For Alavi, the state, in the postcolonial context, rather than simply representing the interests of the business class (national bourgeoisie), as is true for classical Marxist theory, mediates the interests of three propertied classes including national capital (local businesses), foreign capital (metropolitan bourgeoisie or multinationals, the most powerful) and landlords. When Alavi was writing, the landlords were predominantly the political class due to adult franchise and low urbanization in postcolonial societies.[25]

Alavi forwards the concept of relative autonomy to indicate that the state mediates the interests of the three propertied classed and protects their common interest of reproducing the social order. Postcolonial societies inherited a military and bureaucracy that had protected the interests of the colonial power, but being comparatively developed and efficient institutions were able to step into a vacuum in Pakistan's case, as explained earlier, and become a predominant part of the state apparatus.[26] These institutions have maintained their power even when assemblies are functioning. Based on institutional land grants, business interests developed through influence and corruption and intermarriages. The upper echelons of both institutions became part of the co-mingled propertied classes if they were not drawn from them (rarely drawn from the bourgeois class). Hence, the interests of these two governing institutions are closely aligned with the propertied classes, but they maintain relative autonomy to mediate interests based on the policy vision that prevails at a point in time.

Alavi (1983, 62) does not begin with an explicit definition of the state but one can infer this from various phrases such as the state being "an arena for class struggle" or "an institution for the imposition of class rule." This is also the case with other Pakistani state theorists like Jalal (1990; 1995) who refers to the bureaucracy and the military as "institutions of the state."

Alavi (1983, 72–85) provides a fascinating historical account of how the bureaucracy by 1953 had attained supremacy while the military was still building and consolidating. Jalal (1990, chapters 4 and 5), while differing on causes and on the innate strength of political forces, provides a much more detailed historical account but accepts that state power was captured by the bureaucracy and the military. Scholars suggest that the ascendancy of the bureaucratic-military nexus was historically conditioned. The political entrenchment of the rural-military elite in Punjab was arguably the major inheritance of the Pakistani state. This elite both enjoyed the support of and helped reinforce the power of the civil and military bureaucracies.[27] The colonial practice of subordinating the assemblies (ministers) to the bureaucracy (secretaries) remained unchallenged in Pakistan after 1947.

While the bureaucracy might have consolidated its position first, it did not take long for the military to assert itself as the senior partner. For example, during General Mohammad Ayub Khan's presidency, MLR (Martial Law Regulation) 115, clause 10 (1), prohibited government servants from possessing land exceeding one hundred acres, but clause 10 (3) exempted all branches of the military from this restriction.[28] It was during Ayub Khan's rule that the military inserted itself in civilian life including in the bureaucracy. While Prime Minister Zulfiqar Ali Bhutto most effectively undermined the power of the bureaucracy (Civil Service Pakistan) with "lateral entry," converting a closed system to an open one, it was General Zia-ul-Haq who capitalized on this by staffing 10 percent of all posts in the bureaucracy with serving or retired military officers; dictating that this privilege was not to be extended to civilians. Alavi (1983, 67) noted that ex-military generals were favored as heads of state corporations, their preferred appointments, or in critical posts in ministries that controlled appointments and transfers. General Musharraf carried the subordination of the bureaucracy to the extreme by appointing military monitoring committees to oversee bureaucratic functioning.[29]

Jalal (1990, 139) documents that the military started intervening on foreign policy (in favor of an alliance with the US) and the economy (welfare for ex-servicemen) as early as 1951. Showing contempt for parliament, the military had started dealing directly with foreign governments for military aid. Most telling is a statement quoted by Jalal (1990, 175) made by the Commander-in-Chief General Mohammad Ayub Khan to the American consul general in Lahore. In early 1952, a day after the release of the report of the Basic Principles Committee on the framing of the constitution, he is quoted as saying that "the Pakistan Army [would] not allow the political leaders" or the people of Pakistan "to get out of hand."[30]

The bureaucracy as regulators and executors had, and continue to have, nuisance value, and the proliferation of regulations enhanced this nuisance value and enabled their enrichment.[31] However, as one very senior bureaucrat told us during our fieldwork when we were soliciting data, "they have a very long memory." The reference is to the institutional memory of the military and, notwithstanding General Musharraf's crude monitors, they have become ever more sophisticated in exercising control.

Alavi and Jalal also refer to a "state apparatus," and this would presumably mean the institutional structures that embody decision-making and draw from the senior echelons of the bureaucracy, military and parliament (when active). Again, our contention is that the real state apparatus is the GHQ and associated joint service committees and implementing agencies. An ex-head of the Inter Service Intelligence (ISI) openly spoke to a BBC interviewer about trying to influence an election against the PPP and said that this was done in the national interest.[32] Thus, the military has from the inception of the state decided that defining the national interest was its prerogative rather than that of the people's representatives.

During ostensibly democratic periods, as is currently the case (2008–), the military effectively exercises a veto on crucial state policy. Hence, President Asif Ali Zardari was not able to budge on key foreign policy issues such as Afghanistan. While generals nominally negotiate the budget with the cabinet, they are likely to get what they want. For example, the government's Budget in Brief document suggests that for the fiscal year 2010–11, "the defense budget was almost 30 percent more than the budget estimates and 13 percent more than the revised defense budget of the current financial year," notwithstanding the headline complaints of the finance minister in the same daily.[33] More generally, the state does the bidding of the military, as we will document in detail in chapter 7 in a case study of the struggle of the peasantry against their military landlords.

As mentioned at the outset of this section, the theoretical insights offered by Alavi – and other theorists and historians of the Pakistani state – focus only on the relations between dominant institutional and class interests, and do not probe how and why such a configuration of power gains a measure of legitimation from below. Indeed, this lack of emphasis on legitimation is the primary shortcoming of all major analyses of military dominance in Pakistan – not to mention descriptive ones. The prototypical analysis explains the gradual assumption of power by the military in terms of the generation of elite consensus. The military's ability to mediate between both external powers and propertied classes within society underlies its rise, starting even before it assumed the direct reins of government under Ayub Khan. The generation of elite consensus is chronologically documented, with unprecedented accumulation of power and capital taking place during the Zia and Musharraf military regimes, and the democratic interregnums viewed as periods of strategic or temporary retreat.

We argue that it is necessary to augment this well-established explanatory framework with an understanding of the importance of ideology, socialization and generation of consent from below. Our specific emphasis on Punjab underlines the fault lines that run through Pakistani society *vis-à-vis* the military's role – it is in Punjab that a unique social contract was forged in the colonial period which has facilitated the military's growing power and influence in the postcolonial period. In contrast, the military's ability to generate consent in Sindh, Balochistan and what is now Khyber-Pakhtunkhwa has been far more limited. Whereas even within Punjab the seeds of discontent are growing, particularly in Siraiki-speaking areas. It is the question of legitimation – how was it historically generated, in which areas and whether it is now breaking down – which interests us and which we believe is necessary to interrogate to fully comprehend the nature and scale of the military's interventions in Pakistan's agrarian society.[34]

Conclusion

It has been well established in the historical literature that the British used the military and the bureaucracy to enforce and facilitate colonial rule and purpose. Historical circumstances, the lack of an organized political party channeling and empowering popular sentiment as a countervailing force and other factors enabled them to assume state power in Pakistan. They helped the fledgling state to endure, but the upper echelons mostly from the Punjab, who rarely came from propertied classes, ensured, through state land grants and other means including apparent corruption, their continued enrichment. This provided these two institutions with a bigger stake in the social order they used the state apparatus to sustain. We argue that very early on in the history of the country, the military subordinated the bureaucracy to its own purpose and became the seat of power and hence essentially the arbiter of the state.

We show that one very important reason for the military to become ascendant was the state–society consensus on such a dispensation in the Punjab, Pakistan's most populous and richest province. We explain how historical forces and cultural dispositions led a large cross section of Punjabi agriculturalists to accept and tolerate military dominance. We will spend the rest of this book interrogating the extent to which this state–society consensus is now eroding as a result of military high-handedness and its avaricious resource grab.

Any fundamental democratization of the system would affect military interest and is therefore difficult to achieve given that the institution's power and control of the state and ideological apparatus. While this might sound pessimistic, historically a reversal of the hold of nondemocratic power and control can be quite rapid when confronted with mass mobilization. Within a decade after the turn of the century, the seemingly unmovable military in Turkey, on which the Pakistan military seems to have modeled itself, has had to back off in a face down with political forces. That this happened despite the fact that the military is avidly secular and the political majority has recently evinced a more religious orientation.

If there were to be an erosion of the state–society consensus on the military's dominance and economic role, such a reversal would be possible and even likely in Pakistan. The strengthening of political forces based on a popular mandate has enabled the repeal of the 17th Amendment of the Constitution and has restored, in principle, the supremacy of Parliament.[35] This includes the repeal of Article 58 (2) b that deprives the presidency of discretionary powers to dissolve the National Assembly and appoint armed forces chiefs and provincial governors: the mechanism via which the military exercised control.[36] More needs to be done to make the parliament sovereign. And an erosion of the state–society consensus on the guardianship of the military would strengthen the hand of elected representatives in gradually making the necessary moves to strengthen democracy by confining the military solely to its constitutionally mandated role of defense.[37]

Throughout the remaining chapters of this book we will continue to explore whether or not the state–society consensus in Punjab on the military's role is breaking down, using the military's land acquisitions in the province as a case study. Whether over the course of time erosion of this consensus will develop into a coherent political challenge to the military's economic and political power is a matter of conjecture. It could be that the level of co-option within the Punjab remains sufficient to preclude such a political rupture. Or it could be that Punjabis make common cause with non-Punjabis – including Siraikis in the much less developed regions of the province – that are clamoring louder than ever for a renegotiated social contract. [38]

Notes

1 The colonial project in the Punjab was premised upon the firm belief that the northwest frontier of India was the crucial buffer that would protect the vast British Empire – extending as far east as Australia and New Zealand – from potential aggressors to the west and the north. Thus it was from Punjab and the North West Frontier Province (NWFP, now Khyber-Pukhtunkhwa) that the British drew most of their military recruits from around the 1880s onwards. The building of cantonments had far-reaching economic effects, and Punjab also featured the highest density of railroad track in the subcontinent and a formidable road infrastructure (Dewey 1988, 138).

2 This amounts to 8.2 per 1000 persons compared to 3.9 for India. See: http://en.wikipedia.org/wiki/List_of_countries_by_number_of_troops. Sources cited at the bottom of the table.

3 Ali suggests that a hydraulic society is one in which "patterns of dominance and subordination are pervaded by the fact that the water that sustains cropping comes not from the heavens but through human agency and human control."

4 Cheema et al. (2006) make this distinction.

5 See Pasha (1998).

6 We cannot expound at length on the rising tide of Siraiki nationalism, although we do believe the future of Punjab, Pakistan and the military's role in both will be determined in part by the Siraiki question. For a discussion on the history, present and potential future of Siraiki nationalism, see Langah (2011).

7 Also refer to Low's (2002, 262–64) account of Ranjit Singh's very effective development of a military-fiscal state in the Punjab and of how the British continued to use this following the conquest of the Punjab after Ranjit Singh's death. He argues that this "very close conjuncture developed [in the Punjab], as nowhere else in India, between provincial and military administrations" was a crucial colonial legacy that shaped Pakistan's political development. For a detailed comparative analysis of political development in Bangladesh, India and Pakistan refer to Jalal (1995).

8 The electoral regime in Punjab was deliberately crafted to ensure that the latent oppositional tendencies of urban areas were subordinated to the proestablishment vote of the rural areas. More generally, the British expanded democratic institutions in India such that democratic urges could be contained and ensnared in institutions which served the colonial state's needs; thus they were incapable of providing launching pads for broader oppositional politics and were controllable through networks of resource distribution (Washbrook 1990, 42).

9 In the Chenab colony, the biggest of the eight colonies settled by the British, seminomadic pastoralists, or *janglis*, were allotted 448,000 acres of land, or what amounted to 24 percent of total allotment in the colony (Ali 1988, 52).

10 In local parlance this division is framed in the language of *zamindar* and *kammi*. The British institutionalized this division in Punjab through the Land Alienation Act of 1900, which prohibited nonagricultural castes – *kammis* – from owning land. Social and economic changes have had transformational effects on Punjabi society and on

historical caste divisions especially. Nevertheless, the distinction between *zamindars* and *kammis* remains a significant one in Punjab. For a comprehensive account of the manner in which the colonial state politicized caste, see Dirks (2001).

11 The role of external powers, particularly the United States, in reinforcing this unique conflagration of interests in which the military eventually rose to a dominant position was significant (see Jalal 1990).

12 The most obvious example of this shared understanding of politics and administration was the induction of the first indigenous commander-in-chief of the army, General Mohammad Ayub Khan, into the 1954 cabinet as minister of defence; the civil bureaucracy and complicit politicians clearly did not see the need to make the army subservient to civilian authority.

13 Also refer to chapter one on how changing definitions, for example, excluding pensions from defense expenditure during General Pervez Musharraf's regime, understates the military's share.

14 Waseem (2002, 267) points out: "In spatial terms, those regions which were not fully represented in the mainstream politics of the Pakistan movement, or failed to move to centre stage in the emerging State system, did not necessarily share what is otherwise billed as national consensus," implying that the anti-India sentiment was concentrated amongst Punjabis and Muhajirs, and by extension in urban areas of Sindh and Punjab.

15 Resistance of local communities to migrant settlers was much more acute in Sindh where the migrants – both Urdu-speakers in the years following partition and Punjabis that had been allotted agricultural lands in upper Sindh before and after partition – were much more distinct from ethnic Sindhis. See Ansari (2005).

16 Jones (2003, 205) is correct in recognizing that the popular movements of the late 1960s, while influenced greatly by revolutionary slogans, were ultimately "nationalist, participatory, and economic." It should be recalled that the anti-Ayub mobilizations started following the Tashkent declaration, which was widely decried as a sell-out. Bhutto rode a hypernationalist anti-Indian sentiment into power and throughout his time in government. Bhutto (1969) himself claimed India to have a pathological hatred for Pakistan's existence and he in turn manifested a strong anti-Indian sentiment.

17 See Moore (1969) for a perspective that celebrates the military's role in nation building.

18 Colonel Sher Ali was a trusted aide of General Agha Mohammad Yahya Khan, the country's second military dictator. See Siddiqi (1995).

19 Ul Haq (1963) first pointed to the concentration of wealth and income in Pakistan, particularly with his celebrated speech on the 22 industrial groups in April 1968, cited by Power (2006, 270).

20 Military expenditures in 1974 reached an all-time high of 8.4 percent of GDP; in no year since Pakistan's founding had military expenditure been higher than 7.2 percent (Hashmi 1983, 105).

21 Alavi (1982) notes that even the negative effects of the Green Revolution on smallholders and landless peasants were less acute in Punjab – and within the canal colony regions in Punjab – than in other provinces.

22 For a robust analysis of the measurement of Pakistan's diverse middle classes, see Nayab (2011).

23 Punjab certainly has its share of poor districts. However, in a national ranking of social development, closely associated with economic development, eight out of the top 10 districts in the country in the 1990s were in the Punjab (see Ghaus et al. 1996).

24 See, for example, Alavi (1972, 1982 and 1983).

25 In other research, we found that this continues to be true in Pakistan. The landlords by virtue of their landed power, patronage, knowledge of rural areas and brute force continue to dominate legislative assemblies (see Khan, Khan and Akhtar (2007).

26 Jalal (1990, 295) contests this concept of a vacuum, since political forces reflecting popular sentiment might have been contained but were present and manifested themselves in various ways. Instead, she attributes the bureaucratic-military ascendency to a complex set of circumstances including domestic (center-provincial tensions), regional (Indian hostility, near and Middle Eastern politics) and international factors (conflicting British and US maneuvering to secure strategic Pakistani support for their Middle East policies) and resource scarcity that strengthened the military at the expense of development and the political process.

27 Jalal (1995, 51) argues that the desire to keep the Bengali majority at bay, inevitable in a federal structure, urged the Punjabi landed gentry to repress their own provincial and party political leanings and succumb to the centralizing bureaucratic-military nexus, an alliance they certainly gained from.

28 This is consistent with the Mian Mumtaz Daultana's attempt as Punjub's chief minister in 1950 to institute agrarian reform that included abolishing *jagirs* (large landed estates), but the holdings by military or ex-military personnel were exempted (see Jalal 1990, 149).

29 While General Yahya Khan also instituted a system of parallel military officers at all levels of the bureaucracy, this was quickly withdrawn (Alavi, 70). General Zia-ul-Haq and General Pervez Musharraf, to a lesser extent, relied on the military as their constituencies and so the militarization of civilian life and the patronage system to secure loyalty was much more extensive and intensive than under the first two dictators.

30 Subsequent events demonstrated that this was not an idle threat.

31 As the controllers of the police, the bureaucracy has teeth, but the police are toothless, as has been repeatedly demonstrated in Pakistan's history, in the face of superior military training and armaments.

32 The Director General ISI in 1990, General Asad Durrani, openly acknowledged doling out crores of rupees to anti-PPP politicians in the 1990 election campaign so as to influence the outcome of the election (Haqqani 2005). Retired Air Marshall Asghar Khan filed a writ petition in the Supreme Court in 1998 demanding disclosure and punitive action. On 19 October 2012, the Short-Order of the Supreme Court vindicated the air marshall, ordered the closure of election cells maintained by the Military Intelligence (MI), Inter-Services Intelligence or in the Presidency and for the secret funds maintained to be transferred. See http://tribune.com.pk/story/453773/asghar-khan-case-short-order-full-text.

33 See *The Tribune Express*, 6 June 2010, http://tribune.com.pk/story/19101/half-of-the-budget-allocated-to-defence-debt-servicing/.

34 A more detailed exposition of the basic arguments made in this section can be found in Akhtar (2010).

35 That most in Parliament are widely viewed as betraying the popular trust and only seeking the spoils of office is a separate research issue. The important issue is for the preservation of institutions via which the public can discipline those elected to serve them, if only initially by throwing them out of office, is critical for the political process to gradually mature.

36 Political representatives in Pakistan need to be as vigilant against a prime minister making a grab for absolute authority, such as in the case of Zulfiqar Ali Bhutto or

Nawaz Sharif during his second term in office. The latter demonstrated more political maturity in his most recent stint in opposition (2007–2013) than earlier on and this no doubt had a bearing on the peaceful transfer of power from one civilian government to another for the first time in Pakistan's history – perhaps there was a lesson here and in Pakistan's past political history for the Egyptian political opposition to an elected government.

37 Prime Minister Yusuf Raza Gilani was unable to abolish as he vowed the National Security Council, which institutionalizes the role of the military in matters of the state by giving representation to the service chiefs. After he fired a retired military general for speaking out of turn in January 2009, the Council was moved to the presidency with the president rather than the prime minister as chair. This may have something to do with the conciliatory president being the chair of the party that the prime minister belonged to, but we believe the prime minister's instincts on this issue were correct for the strengthening of democracy. A much more serious confrontation took place between the prime minister and the military establishment over the infamous 'memogate' case pertaining to preempting a suspected military takeover (see http://en.wikipedia.org/wiki/Memogate). Such public challenges by political representatives are part of challenging the military's dominance. In this context, seeing through the treason case against General Musharraf for abrogating the constitution is critical.

38 Crucially, some of the newest and more egregious military land allotment schemes are unfolding in Siraiki areas in which new irrigation schemes are being designed and executed.

References

Akhtar, A. S. 2010. "Pakistan: Crisis of a Frontline State." *Journal of Contemporary Asia* 40 (1), 105–22. London: Routledge.

Alavi, H. 1990. "Authoritarianism and Legitimation of State Power in Pakistan." *The Post-Colonial State in Asia: Dialectics of Politics and Culture.* New York: Harvester Wheatsheaf.

_____. 1987. "Pakistan and Islam: Ethnicity and Ideology." In *State and Ideology in the Middle East and Pakistan.* New York: Monthly Review Press.

_____. 1983. "Class and State." *Pakistan: The Unstable State.* Lahore: Vanguard Books.

_____. 1982. "The Rural Elite and Agricultural Development in Pakistan." *Pakistan: The Political Economy of Rural Development.* Lahore: Vanguard Books.

_____. 1972, "The State in Post-Colonial Societies: Pakistan and Bangladesh." *New Left Review* 74, 59–81.

Ali, I. 1988. *Punjab under Imperialism.* Karachi: Oxford University Press.

Ansari, S. 2005. *Life after Partition: Migration, Community and Strife in Sindh, 1947–1962.* Karachi: Oxford University Press.

Bhutto, Z. A. 1969. *The Myth of Independence.* New York: Oxford University Press.

Cheema, A., S. Mohmand and A. Asad. 2006. "History, Land Settlement and Semi-Formal Local Governance Structures in Sargodha." *Working Paper.* Lahore: Lahore University of Management Sciences.

Cheema, P. I. 2003. *The Armed Forces of Pakistan.* London: Orion.

Cohen, S. P. 1998. *The Pakistan Army.* Karachi: Oxford University Press.

Dewey, C. 1991. "The Rural Roots of Pakistani Militarism." *The Political Inheritance of Pakistan.* Basingstoke: Macmillan.

_____. 1988. *Arrested Development in India: The Historical Dimension*. London: Riverdale.

Dirks, N. 2001, *Castes of Mind: Colonialism and the Making of Modern Caste*. Durham: Duke University Press.

Ghaus, A. 1996. "Social Development Ranking of Districts of Pakistan." *The Pakistan Development Review* 35 (4), 593–614.

Hashmi, B. 1983. "Dragon Seed: Military in the State." *Pakistan: The Unstable State*. Lahore: Vanguard Books.

Jalal, A. 1995. *Democracy and Authoritarianism in South Asia: A Comparative and Historical Perspective*. Cambridge: Cambridge University Press.

_____. 1990. *The State of Martial Rule: The Origins of Pakistan's Political Economy of Defense*. Cambridge: Cambridge University Press.

Javid, H. 2011. "Class, Power and Patronage: Landowners and Politics in Punjab." *History and Anthropology* 22 (3), 337–69.

Jones, P. E. 2003. *The Pakistan People's Party: Rise to Power*. Karachi: Oxford University Press.

Khan, S. R., F. S. Khan and A. S. Akhtar,. 2007. *Initiating Devolution for Service Delivery in Pakistan: Forgetting the Power Structure*. Karachi: Oxford University Press.

Langah, N. T. 2011. *Poetry as Resistance: Islam and Ethnicity in Postcolonial Pakistan*. Abingdon: Routledge.

Low, D. A. 2002, "Pakistan and India: Political Legacies from the Colonial Past." *South Asian Studies* 25 (2), 257–72.

Nayab, D. 2011, "Estimating the Middle Class in Pakistan," Unpublished paper. Islamabad: Pakistan Institute of Development Economics.

Pasha, M. K. 1998. *Colonial Political Economy: Recruitment and Underdevelopment in the Punjab*. Karachi: Oxford University Press.

Power, M., 2006. "Mahbub Ul Haq." *Fifty Key Thinkers on Development*. New York: Routledge.

Rizvi, H. A. 2003. *Military, State and Society*. Lahore: Sang-e-Meel.

Shafqat, S. 1997. *Civil-Military Relations in Pakistan: From Zulfikar Ali Bhutto to Benazir Bhutto*. Boulder: Westview Press.

Siddiqi, A. R. 1996. *The Military in Pakistan: Image and Reality*. Karachi: Vanguard Books.

Tan, T. Y. 2005. *The Garrison State: Military, Government and Society in Colonial Punjab, 1849–1947*. London: Sage.

Tan, T. Y. 1995. "Punjab and the Making of Pakistan: The Roots of Civil-Military State." *South Asia* 18 (1), 177–92.

Ul Haq, M. 1963. *The Strategy of Economic Planning: A Case Study of Pakistan*. Karachi: Oxford University Press.

Waseem, M. 2003. "Mohajirs in Pakistan: A Case of Nativisation of Migrants." *Community, Empire and Migration: South Asian in Diaspora*. Delhi: Orient Longman.

Waseem, M. 2002. "The Dialectic of Domestic Policy and Foreign Policy." *Pakistan: Nationalism without a Nation*. London: Zed Books.

Waseem, M. 1999. "Partition of Punjab: A Comparative Study of Migration and Assimilation." *Partition and Region: Punjab and Bengal*. Karachi: Oxford University Press.

Washbrook, D. 1997. "The Rhetoric of Democracy and Development in Late Colonial India." *Nationalism, democracy and development: state and politics in India*. Delhi: Oxford University Press.

Zaidi, S A. 2005. "State, Military and Social Transition: Improbable Future of Democracy in Pakistan." *Economic and Political Weekly* 40 (49), 5173–81.

Chapter Three

RESEARCH DESIGN, METHOD, INSTITUTIONAL ISSUES AND SCOPE OF THE MILITARY'S LAND ACQUISITIONS

Introduction

There are three kinds of military agrarian land acquisitions in the Punjab: individual border-land allocations, other individual welfare-land allocations, and collective land allocations such as for a stud farm. As documented in the previous chapter, the practice of allotting land to military personnel in irrigated districts of Punjab has a long history. With the inception of the new state, this practice continued, with General Ayub Khan's regime initiating allotment schemes on the eastern border with India. This process intensified with each new military regime and with General Musharraf they reached a new high in the form of nonborder allocations in districts in the Siraiki belt such as Bahawalpur, Layyah and Bhakkar. Even collective land allocations are often reduced to individual allocations, as indicated in chapters 4 and 5. Unless otherwise specified, the two broad categories we work with in this, and the next two, chapters are border and nonborder allocations. Allocations vary positively across the military hierarchy by rank.[1]

The military's agrarian interventions are in both the Punjab and Sindh provinces. We focused on the Punjab because it is here that a distinct state–society consensus has been forged (see chapter 2). In the rest of this chapter, we explain our evolving research design and method, and outline the institutional issues pertinent to our research including the conceptualization of the border allotment scheme, the allocation process, legal issues including those pertaining to civil-military conflict and border Rangers and police jurisdiction issues. We follow with information on the scope of the nonborder allocations and end with a preview of the field research based chapters that follow.

An Evolving Research Design and Method

We originally intended to focus only on the border allocation scheme and to select a stratified random sample. The border allotments are made in a five-mile belt all along the Indian–Pakistan border. In Punjab, this starts from Sialkot district in the north and ends with Rahim Yar Khan district to the south. The interim districts are Narowal, Sheikhupura, Lahore, Kasur, Okara, Bahawalnagar and Bahawalpur. Not all land in this five-mile belt has been allocated and some of the land originally owned in this belt is under civilian ownership.

We expected to pick one district in northern and one in southern Punjab and subsequently randomly select *tehsils*, union councils, *patwari halqas*[2] (land they maintain records for) and farms as the unit of analysis. We hoped to get a sampling frame from the Border Area Committee (BAC) office that deals with border allocations. When the colonel who serves as chairman blankly refused to provide any information, stating it was confidential, we ascertained that we could get this information from the copies of allocations retained by the Punjab Board of Revenue. However, we were not successful here either. Undeterred, we decided to use a geographical map as the sampling frame and accordingly move down to a selection of districts, *tehsils*, union councils, *patwaris*, and farms as the unit of analysis.

We expected to identify military farms, and using a control group (nonmilitary farm of the same size) study issues of efficiency, tenure, treatment of cultivators and possible asymmetrical access to, and abuse of, state resources. We pretested the research instruments (questionnaires) in the field and found that our quantitative focus was unlikely to yield much for both kinds of allocations.

First, each district has from two to six *tehsils*, each *tehsil* from four to six union councils and each union council from one to five *patwari halqas*. Given our limited time and budget, we were unlikely to get many relevant farms in our sample from random selection. Second, not all *tehsils*, union councils and *halqas* were relevant from the perspective of military allocations and our random selection may not have yielded much. Third, we discovered during the pretests that *patwaris* are not amenable to random selection. Securing information from them is a challenging endeavor and the recommendation of friends and acquaintances, preferably of those who have leverage, is often necessary. Fourth, and most important, many military men had either not claimed their land (below officer level) or sold it, and those that had retained ownership were mostly contracting out on a fixed-rent basis. Hence, most of the tenure questionnaires and the access questionnaires we had developed were irrelevant.

We realized that we needed to maximize exposure to those areas in which allotments to military personnel had been made and land actually claimed.

Thus, our focus shifted away from quantitative and comparative questions towards a more qualitative and suggestive study. In this vein, we also realized that exploring just the border allocations would be too limiting. We therefore broadened the scope of the research study to include all military land allocations in the Punjab. In any case, it became clear within a fairly short period after we began our research that it is in nonborder areas, particularly in southern and western parts of the province, in which population density is lower and agricultural cultivation less intense, that the majority of new allotments are taking place. Allotments in highly arid, virtual desert zones such as Thal and Cholistan began in the 1950s and then intensified in later decades following the creation of the Thal Development Authority (TDA) and Cholistan Development Authority (CDA) respectively. It is in these regions that most of the current allotments are being made because there is no longer that much available land in the canal irrigated districts of central Punjab.

In a nutshell, we ended up pursuing whatever lead we could find based on all the contacts we could muster to gather information and data relevant to our research questions. In the climate of fear that prevails regarding the military, we were often unable to solicit responses without contacts when randomly approaching any particular group of villages. Having started with a purist sample design constructed far from the field to yield statistically random data with which we would test economic hypothesis on farm efficiency (military vs nonmilitary), our methods and design changed considerably and the study became far more of an exploratory one. In broad terms, we decided to explore social impacts and responses to the military's land acquisitions and relate these to the themes of social justice and social consensus identified in chapters 1 and 2. We added to these broad research questions in a spirit of learning by doing as our fieldwork progressed. For example, early on in the research process we found that paramilitary Rangers patrolling the border were an integral part of the military's burgeoning corporate empire (see chapter 4).

Thus, from structured and semistructured questionnaires, our research method evolved to relying on key informant interviews and farmer and citizen group discussions. All the key informant interviews and group discussions were based on existing contacts; additional contacts were generated during the course of the initial meetings via a snowball method. For the border allocations, we covered all the districts in the Punjab, though not all the *tehsils*. We used the same research method to explore nonborder interventions and the military's collective allocations. In the case of nonborder allocations, we cannot claim exhaustive coverage – we targeted what we thought were the most conspicuous examples in terms of scale, as well as political controversy and reaction generated.

Our pretest fieldwork spanned from 31 May 2010 to 11 June 2010. This included trips to the provincial capital for data and institutional information, and the field test of instruments and exploration of data availability was done in Kasur District. By this time, we had determined what the substance of our research was going to be. The second intensive phase of the fieldwork that included six field trips continued until 21 July 2010. The third and less intensive phase of the fieldwork continued until the end of February 2011. In subsequent months, until the time that the book was first submitted for review, we continued to follow popular media reports and investigate interesting new leads wherever it was logistically feasible to do so. The list of districts and *tehsils* visited for border and nonborder allocations is in appendix 3.1, the list of persons consulted and interviewed is included as appendix 3.2, the list of group discussions as appendix 3.3, an example of recent military allocations made by the Punjab Board of Revenue as appendix 3.4, examples of nonborder allocations made in Cholistan as appendix 3.5 and a map indicating our coverage as appendix 3.6.

Institutional Issues

Border allocations

Army GHQ (General Headquarters, Rawalpindi) manages border allocations with implementation assistance from the Border Area Committee (BAC) located in the provincial capital, Lahore. BAC also has a field office in Tehsil Bahawalnagar, Bahawalnagar District, for operational assistance. The BAC is headed by a serving colonel and it works closely with the Punjab Board of Revenue which makes the land available to the military for allocations. In fact, the offices of both the chairman of the BAC and the major serving under him are in a Board of Revenue building. We acquired institutional information from the major, because the head of the BAC was either late (arrived after 11:00 a.m.) or absent from work on our visits. Apparently, turnover is high in the BAC office and so institutional information is scarce. We did manage to glean some institutional information from lawyers working with the BAC who we met in the Board of Revenue offices. No documents for any aspect of these allocations were made available to us, although they no doubt exist in GHQ in the form of confidential reports. Since we do not have access to those reports, we have patched together the institutional information as best as possible via discussions with government officials and concerned lawyers.

Conceptualization of the border allocation scheme

The BAC was established in 1952 and initially refugee claims on the border were under its purview. Only civil land ownership on the border established prior to 1952 was, and is, honored by GHQ and the BAC. The border allotments are made in a five-mile belt along Pakistan's eastern international border with India. The idea was to have the barren land made fertile by the military personnel settled there. More importantly, the retired military presence could facilitate the military in time of war. Instead of an unorganized exodus, there would be disciplined leadership managing the civilian population and interfacing with the military.[3]

In proportion to the agricultural allocations, land in *marlas* was made available in nearby towns to facilitate settlement.[4] Initially, the agricultural land had to be retained for five years before it was eligible for sale and a no-objection certificate (NOC) had to be procured from GHQ in such cases. The major informed us that the 1965 and 1971 wars vindicated this border allocation scheme and the military found that their expectations were realized. However, he also conceded that almost 90 percent of allotted land had been sold. While it was impossible for us to verify whether the land in question had been sold before or after the two aforementioned wars, the high proportion of land allocations subsequently sold suggests that the border allocation scheme was a failure, at least in terms of its official stated purpose.

Land allocation process[5]

If GHQ wants to make allocations, it seeks information about state land via the Defense Ministry from the relevant province. For Punjab, the Board of Revenue (BoR) reports on the status of available land and GHQ then makes the allocation, informing the BAC which passes instructions down to the District Coordinator's Office (DCO) and on to revenue officials, starting with the Executive District Officer of Revenue (EDOR) and finally the *patwari* for registration of the plot.[6] A settlement officer of the BoR coordinates with the BAC and has an adjoining office. While information on allocations are considered highly confidential, higher officials at the BoR informed us that copies of allocations are maintained in the settlement office. We managed to secure a copy of allocations since 1999 in a few districts through a senior official in the BoR, details of which are provided in appendix 3.4. It is worth noting that the said official meticulously ensured that the copy provided to us had his name removed from it. We were unable to secure any more official records from the BoR.

Legal issues

One of the BAC's functions is trouble shooting. For example, one plot of land can and has often been allotted several times by GHQ. The BAC investigates such problems and reports back to GHQ. Those who have a genuine prior allotment are not displaced, and in cases where a plot of land is allotted more than once accidentally, GHQ makes a fresh allotment.

We consulted a constitutional lawyer on the issue of constitutional cover for the military border scheme and other land allocations and about which law has primacy if there is conflict between military and civil law. His response was that the consensus view in the legal profession is that martial law is an aberration that suspends the Constitution. Martial Law Regulations (MLRs), providing for such allocations, can be given constitutional cover, via indemnity, when civilian law is restored.

The BAC also functions as a court. Two army officers and a junior member of the Punjab BoR form the bench. For example, a plot of land might be sold without an NOC from GHQ and issues pertaining to that plot of land could be adjudicated on by the BAC. In general, such land was reappropriated by the BAC with a loss to the buyer and the land reallocated to military personnel. Lawyers were resentful that the chairman of the BAC, who presides in the hearing, is high handed, "acts like a sovereign" and refuses to make relevant files available to litigants, and views this court as "subject to approach" (corrupt).

Decisions of bodies such as the BAC, which have legal recognition, can in principle be challenged under Article 166 of the Constitution via a writ petition (when all recourse is exhausted), with petitioners having the right to seek legal counsel. Civil courts have rarely provided relief to ordinary civilians. In principle, writ petitions on the BAC cases could eventually make their way up the civilian court system and be filed by litigants in the Lahore High Court. Two senior judges of the division bench heard the case. Lawyers engaged in the BAC litigation informed us that that the High Court often remanded (sent back) the cases to lower courts. If the civil courts did decide against retired military personnel selling the land illegally, and if the sale was nullified, military personnel would in principle have to compensate the buyers for the amount taken. This rarely happened in practice, since the BAC did not recognize the jurisdiction of civilian courts – it would later reappropriate the land and reallocate it.

All this is now moot, since in 2008 the Supreme Court declared that an NOC is not required unless the buyer is deemed by some competent authority to be an "undesirable." This has legally converted the Border Land Allotment into a welfare scheme like the nonborder allotments, which it de facto was in any case.

More importantly, the very fact that the GHQ can arbitrarily demand information on available state land from the provincial authorities and then instruct the same authorities to simply allot this land to military officers, without concern for what alternative uses may have been imagined by the civil authorities, including elected representatives, reflects just how much power the military actually exercises *vis-à-vis* other state institutions. Many of our informants expressed resentment at just how unashamedly this practice has become institutionalized and how little resistance there is to it on the part of other state institutions.

We turn to the activities of Rangers in the next chapter. A brief note is necessary here to clarify the legal status of the institution. The Rangers are the border guardians, but they do not have policing authority except on issues of border crossings and related defense concerns. However, since the police are obliged to accept the Rangers' view of matters on any law and order issue, the latter exercise considerable additional authority over locals beyond policing the cutting of trees that are deemed a defense asset (cover for tanks and other vehicles). Using intimidation and claims that troublemakers are Indian agents or smugglers, and with the ability to block farming activity under some pretext, Rangers generally get their way.

Scope of Nonborder Allocations

The macro picture

Siddiqa (2007, 174–82) reports that about 12 percent of state land is in military hands. The appropriations are based on the Colonization of Land Act, 1912, and made by the provincial governments on the request of the military via the Ministry of Defense. Almost two-thirds of all allocations are rural and 98.5 percent of total allocation are private (retired military) ownership, both border and nonborder. The rest include camping grounds, oats, hay, and dairy and stud farms.

As stated at the outset of this chapter, the information we gathered on border and nonborder allotments is not exhaustive. However, while it is at least possible to identify the general contours of the border allotment scheme, nonborder allotments are potentially much broader. As documented in the previous chapter, allotments throughout the so-called canal colonies have been ongoing for the best part of a century. In traditional allotment districts such as Okara, Sahiwal, Khanewal, Faisalabad, Sargodha and Multan there is now only limited land that remains to be allotted.[7] Thus it is in the Siraiki-speaking southern and western districts that most new allotments are taking place. In most cases, it is common lands, or what are locally known as *rakh* (previously used mostly as grazing lands), that have been acquired by the state and allotted to military (and other government) personnel. This practice is not necessarily new, but it is these lands which appear to have become the favoured targets of GHQ allotment schemes in districts such as Layyah, Muzaffargarh, Bahawalpur and Dera Ghazi Khan.

The lands in question are variously irrigated and rain fed; it is largely in the districts of the Thal desert such as Layyah and Muzaffargarh that rain-fed lands have been allotted. There are also a number of new mega water-projects, either in the planning or execution stages, which command areas in the millions of acres. Crucially, the main planning document (PC-1) that outlines the design execution plan of these projects – which include the Greater Thal Canal (GTC) and the Chashma Right Bank Canal (CRBC) – leaves vague the question of who the beneficiaries of the new irrigated land will be. In the event, in both the case of the GTC (which had not been completed at the time of writing) and the CRBC (which is complete), we found plenty of anecdotal evidence to suggest that new colonists include a large number of military personnel.

In the Cholistan region, and most notably in Bahawalpur, where we found the most allotments, a number of trends can be discerned. First, there are non-negligible lands that have been allotted that have no access to water. We can only presume that there is a prospective plan to provide water access to such lands in the future. Second, there are a number of allotments that appear to have been made for urban expansion – so nominally rural (periurban) allotments in and around Bahawalpur city will be subsumed into the cantonment area, a model of development which, as we noted in chapter 2, has colonial roots. Third, military allottees have benefited from the abuse of power to divert existing water sources to their lands. Many of the irrigation initiatives undertaken by the state in the 1950s and 1960s prior to the creation of the CDA were not perennial. In many cases, those who came to the region as land allottees (and this included large numbers of east Punjabi and Urdu-speaking partition migrants along with civil and military personnel) were able to rely on only six months of irrigation water. Anecdotal evidence suggests that many of the more recent military allottees have been able to secure water from the older sources for much more than the typical six-month period. In other words, they have essentially monopolized existing water sources and this has given rise to considerable conflict with the local population that does not have access to perennial irrigation.[8] Finally, there are a number of different types of tenure arrangements in operation. Aside from transfer of ownership to individual allottees, there are long-term leases, short-term leases, sublets (mostly illegal) and even blatantly illegal occupations. Details of some allotment in Cholistan to the military are provided in appendix 3.5.[9]

Preview

The rest of the book documents field research based findings and ends with a summary of these findings. Chapters 4 and 5 are based on the fieldwork done for this book. Chapters 6 and 7 are more detailed case studies based on separate but related fieldwork. In chapter 4 we focus on the perceptions of the locals who experience the impact of military-land acquisitions on a daily basis. We document the predatory practices of the border Rangers and show that the predation at the macro level by the military is replicated on the micro level.

In chapter 5 we document the social resentment and resistance resulting from the military's land acquisitions. As in chapter 4, we narrate what we gleaned from several sources using key informants and group discussions. The negative perceptions that we document are the basis of the social resistance that we document and this may be the start of the erosion of the social consensus (refer to chapter 2) that enables the military to grab a disproportionate amount of state resources.

Chapters 6 and 7 are much more detailed case studies than those presented in chapters 4 and 5. In chapter 6, following the research method adopted for chapters 4 and 5, we document the military's involvement in the real-estate business in the periurban areas and how this has led to social injustice. In chapter 7 we explore in detail the well-known case of peasant resistance to the military as a landlord in Okara, Punjab, which occurred in 2000. This reinforces our contention concerning the erosion of the social consensus that emerged from findings documented in chapter 5.

Appendices to Chapter 3

Appendix 3.1. List of the visited districts of Punjab

Border districts

District visited	Number of *tehsils* and union councils	Villages and towns visited
Sialkot	4 *tehsils*: Sialkot, Daska, Pasrur, Sambrial. Total union councils: 124.	Tehsil Sialkot-Umranwali, Faiz Pur.
Shaikhupura	5 *tehsils*: Sheikhupura, Ferozwala, Muridke, Sharaqpur, Safdarabad. Total union councils: 112.	Tehsil Muridke-Meerowal, Kala khatai.
Lahore	2 *tehsils*: Lahore City, Lahore Cant.	Tehsil Lahore Cantt- Ghowind, Chhota Rampura.
Kasur	3 *tehsils*: Kasur, Chonian, Pattoki, Kot Radha Kishen. Total union councils: 141.	Tehsil Chonian-Shahbaz k, Kangan Pur, Kali Snsari Tehsil Kasur-Bhedian Kalan, Sahjra Kalan, Head Ganda Singh.
Okara	3 *tehsils*: Okara, Deepalpur, Renala Khurd. Total union councils: 114.	Tehsil Okara-Coleyana, 27.2/R, 31. 2/R, Tehsil Deepalpur Mahant Darshan, Killi Fojia, Head Sulemaneki, Qandr K, Mhar Baqr.
Bahawalnagar	5 *tehsils*: Bahawalnagar, Minchan Abad, Chishtian, Haroon Abad, Fort Abbas. Total union councils: 118.	Tehsil Minchanabad-Siryanwala, Uraang, Mandi Sadiq ganj, bareka pul. Tehsil Fort Abbas.
Bahawalpur	6 *tehsils*: Bahawalpur City, Bahawalpur Sadar, Yazman, Hasilpur, Ahmadpur, Khairpur Tamianwali. Total union councils: 107.	Tehsil Bahawalpur Khanqa Sharif.
Rahim Yar Khan	4 *tehsils*: Rahim Yar Khan, Khanpur, Sadiq Abad, Liaqatpur. Total union councils: 122.	Tehsil RahimYar Khan-Lakhiwala 101/p. Tehsil Khan Pur-Jatha Putha. 220p, 221p, 224p, 254p (These villages come under the Cholistan Development Authority).
Narowal	2 *tehsils*: Zafar wal, Shakar Garh. Total union councils: 74.	Tehsil Shaker Garh-Wadda Bhai Masroor.

Nonborder districts

Name of district	Number of *tehsils* and union councils	Villages and towns visited
Layyah	3 *tehsils*: Layyah, Chaubara, Karor Lal Esan. Total union councils: 44.	Tehsil Layyah-Kot Sultan, Tehsiil Chaubara Chowk Azam, Rakh kona Nawa Kot.
Muzaffargarh	*4 tehsils*: Muzaffargarh, Kot Adu, Jotoi, Alipur. Total union councils: 93.	Kot Adu Chowk Munda Rakh Azizabad.
Rajanpur	3 *tehsils*: Rajan Pur, Rojhan, Jampur. Total union councils: 44.	Tehsil Rajan Pur-Kotla pehlwan, Feteh Pur, Dhundi estate.
Dera Ghazi Khan	3 *tehsils*: D.G.Khan, Taunsa, Tribal Areas. Total union councils: 59.	Dera Ghazi Khan city.
Khushab	3 *tehsils*: Khushab, Nurpur, Quaidabad. Total union councils: 102.	Khushab Johar Abad.

Appendix 3.2. List of individuals consulted and interviewed in the last six months of 2010[10]

District Bahawal Nagar

1. Adnan Bodla (Social worker and student, District Bahawalnagar)
2. Rao Mudasar (Businessman, District Bahawalnagar)
3. Junaid Ahmad Bodla (Agriculturist, Tehsil Minchan Abad)
4. Nawab Ali (ex-army man, Tehsil Minchanabad)
5. Muhammad Sadiq Joiya (Agriculturist and village elder, Siryanwala, Tehsil Minchanabad)
6. Muhammad Iqbal Kalya (Village elder and farmer, Uraang, Tehsil Minchanabad)
7. Nayeb Tehsildar and two *patwaris* of Tehsil Minchanabad
8. Gharib Ullah Ghazi (Journalist, Fort Abbas)
9. Haji Mukhtar (Farmer, Fort Abbas)
10. Salman Choudhary (Businessman, Fort Abbas)
11. Hafeez Zia (Journalist, Fort Abbas)
12. Station house officer of Fort Abbas

District Bahawalpur

1. Jhangir Mukhlis (Lecturer and poet, Bahawalpur)
2. Hafiz Saleh (Law student, Bahawalpur)
3. Azhar Hussain Pirzada (Lawyer, Bahawalpur)
4. Haji Faqir Ullah (Farmer, Khanqa Sharif)
5. Chairman of the Cholistan Development Authority, Bahawalpur
6. Sarfraz Khan (Advocate, Bahawalpur)

District Kasaur

1. Sardar Sidiq Dogar (Advocate, Tehsil Courts Chonian)
2. Sardar Shareef Dogar (Advocate, District Courts Kasaur)
3. Enayet (Farmer and land renter)
4. Sardar Muhammad Hussain Dogar (Land owner, Shahbaz k, Kangan pur, Tehsil Chonian)
5. Zulkarnain Dogar (Student, Shahbazke, Kanganpur)
6. Sardar Bisharat Dogar (Kanganpur, Tehsil Chonian)
7. Asgher Kamboh (Village elder and activist)

District Lahore

1. Muhammad Rashid (Lecturer, Ghowind, Tehsil Lahore Cantt)
2. Muhammad Sadiq (Farmer, Ghowind)
3. Taj Din (Farmer and *nambrdar*)
4. Malik Sattar (Village elder and farmer)
5. Rahmat Khan(Village elder)
6. Ali Cheema (Associate professor of economics and head of department, Lahore University of Management Sciences, LUMS)
7. Ijaz Nabi (Professor of economics and dean of School of Humanities, Social Sciences and Law, LUMS)
8. Anjum Nasim (Professor of economics and provost, LUMS)

District Rahim Yar Khan

1. Choudhary Kamran (Banker, Rahim Yar Khan)
2. Akbar Kamboh (Agriculurist, 101p Lakhiwala, Tehsil Rahim Yar Khan)
3. Nadeem Noon (Farmer)
4. Haidar Chughtai (Political Worker, Rahim Yar Khan)
5. Jam Ali Asgher (Activist)
6. Mujahid Jatoi (Businessman, Seraiki Nationalist Khanpur)
7. Khalid Dad Chachar (Journalist, activist and lawyer)
8. Basharat Hundal (Advocate, Rahim Yar Khan)
9. Abdur Rashid Chandio (Saraiki poet, Khanpur, Rahim Yar Khan)

District Sialkot

1. Ali Sameer (Businessman)
2. Muhammad Umar (Pharmacist, Fezpur, Tehsil Sialkot)
3. Muhammad Fazil (Village elder, Umranwali, Tehsil Sialkot)

District Narowal

1. Hasnaat Ahmad (Government employee, Tehsil Shakar Garh)
2. Shafqaat Ahmad (Farmer and social worker, Tehsil Shakar Garh)
3. Azhar Bashir (School teacher, Vadda Bhai Masroor, Tehsil Shakar Garh)

District Sheikhupura

1. Muhammad Babar (student, Sheikhupura)
2. Jamal din (Farmer, Meerowal, Tehsil Muridke Meerowal)
3. Ghafoor Ahmad (Farmer, Meerowal)

District Okara

1. Saleem Jhakar (President of local tenants movement, Okara)
2. Ayaz Nasir Jindeka (Advocate, Tehsil Deepalpur)
3. Khurram Waheed (Political worker, Hujra Shah Muqeem, Tehsil Deepalpur)
4. Taj Muhammad (Retired army man, Mhant Darshan)
5. Mian Haq Nawaz Watto (Land owner, businessman, Head Sulemanki, Tehsil Deepalpur)

District Dera Ghazi Khan

1. Hameed Asghar Shaheen (Seraiki nationalist leader, Dera Ghazi Khan)
2. Tashteet Ahmad Bodla (Businessman and social worker, Dera Ghazi Khan)
3. Hasan Raza (NGO Employee)

District Layyah

1. Malik Afzal Jagwal (Advocate, Tehsil Chaubara)

District Muzaffargarh

1. Fazal e Rabbi Lund (Seraiki nationalist, Tehsil Kot Adu)
2. Muhammad Akram Chandio Baloch (School teacher)

District Rajan Pur

1. Rasheed Ahmad Langah(Advocate, Activist Rajanpurur)
2. Kaswar Dareeshak (Government employee, Rajanpur)
3. Sardar Nasar Ullah Dareeshak (Politician, Rajanpur)

District Khushab

1. Sajjad Haidar (Government employee and working for education in Khushab, Joharabad and Islamabad)
2. Malik Laal Khan (Trade and labor union worker, Khushab)

Appendix 3.3. List of the group discussions in the districts visited

District Kasur

02/06/2010
Participants:
    Sardar Muhammad Hussain Dogar (Land owner)
    Sardar Bashart Dogar (Land owner)
    Sardar Waseem Dogar (Land owner)
    Jameel Ahmad Bhatti (Land owner)
    Muhammad Nasir (Land owner)
Place: Village Shahbazke, near Kangan Pur, Tehsil Chonian, District Kasaur

15/12/2010
Participants:
    Sharif Ahmad (Milkman)
    Ashiq Ali (Farmer, activist)
    Shafqat (Shopkeeper).
Place: Village Bhedian Kalaan, near Head Ganda Singh, Tehsil and District Kasaur

15/12/2010
Participants:
    Asgher Kamboh (Village elder and activist)
    Baba Ahmad Ali (Village elder)
    Youth of the village and elders.
Place: Central Square of the village Sahjra Kalaan, near Ganda Singh border, Tehsil and
    District Kasaur.

District Okara

14/6/2010
Participants:
    Saleem Jhakar (Chairman Anjuman e Maza'areen Okara)
    Baba Chandi (Farmer and tenant of army land)
    Farmers and tenants of the village
Place: 27. 2/R Tehsil and District Okara

16/6/2010
Participants:
    Baba Taj (Retired army man)
    Saeed Ahmad Jindeka (Farmer)
    Haji Suleman (Farmer)
    Local villagers
Place: Killi Fojianwali, Tehsil Deepalpur, District Okara

23/6/2010
Participants:
> Mian Haq Nawaz Watto (Farmer, businessman)
> Dr Ameen (Medical practioner, farmer)
> Abdul Hameed (Farmer)
> A bunch of locals

Place: Head Sulemanki Tehsil and District Okara

District Bahawal Nagar

24/6/2010
Participants:
> Mohammad Sadiq Joiya (Village elder)
> Muhammad Iqbal Kalya (Village elder)
> A couple of local villagers of Uraang and Sityanwali Tehsil Minchan Abad

Place: House of Muhammad Iqbal Kalya, village Siryanwali, Tehsil Minchan, Abad District and Bahawal Nagar

06/07/2010
Participants:
> Adnan Sami Bodla
> Rao Mudassar
> Political Workers and civil society members of Bahawal Nagar city

Place: Gulberg Colony, Albarkat Street, Bahawal Nagar City

07/07/2010
Participants:
> Hafeez Zia (Journalist)
> Gharib Ullah Ghazi (Journalist)
> And some local journalists and businessmen of Fort Abbas

Place: Hafeez Zia home that is also a temporary Press club, near main Bazaar Fort Abbas

District Bahawalpur

02/07/2010
Participants:
> Azhar Hussain Peerzada, other lawyers of Bahawal Pur District Courts and some clients.

Place: Peerzada Law Chamber, District Courts Bahawal Pur

District Lahore

30/08/2010
Participants:
> Muhammad Rashid (Lecturer and resident of village) and his brothers
> Taj Din (*Numbrdar* of village Ghowind)
> Muhammad Sadiq (Village elder)

Place: Home of Muhammad Rashid, Village Ghowind, Tehsil Lahore Cantonment, Lahore

01/09/2010
Participants:
  Muhammad Akbar (Village elder)
  Malik Sattar (Farmer and shopkeeper)
  Rahmat Khan (Farmer, *numbrdar*)
  Local youth and a patwari
Place: Central square of village Chhota Rampura, Tehsil Lahore Cantt, Lahore

District Sheikhupura

02/09/2010
Participants:
  Abdul Ghafoor (Village elder and farmer)
  Jamaat Ali (Shopkeeper)
  Village youth, elders and shopkeepers
Place: Village Meerowal, Tehsil and District Sheikhupura

District Narowal

21/07/2010
Participants:
  Shafqaat Ahmad (Farmer)
  Azhar Bashir (School teacher)
  Shop keepers and elders of the village
Place: Village Wadda Bhai Masroor, Tehsil Shakar Garh, District Narowal

District Sialkot

20/07/2010
  Participants:
  Muhammad Fazil (*Numberdar* of village)
  Elders of the village
Place: Main tea bar of village Umranwali, Tehsil and District Sialkot

District Rahim Yar Khan

01/10/2010
Participants:
  Chaudhary Akbar Kamboh and his sons
  Villagers
Place: 101p Lakhiwala, Tehsil and District Rahim Yar Khan

02/10/2010
Participants:
  All participants were local land-owners and they did not want to be named.
Place: At a sitting place of a landlord of village 220p, Tehsil and District Rahim Yar Khan

03/10/2010
Participants:
    Jam Ali Asgher (Seraiki nationalist)
    Abdur Rasheed Dostam Chandio (Seraiki nationalist poet)
    A couple of Seraiki nationalist workers
Place: Main Bazaar, Tehsil Khanpur, District Rahim Yar Khan

04/10/2010
Participants:
    Raees Khaliq Dad Chachar (Lawyer, editor *Bhej Pagara*, Rahim Yar Khan)
    Staff of daily newspaper *Bhej Pagara*, Rahim Yar Khan
Place: Office of daily *Bhej Pagara* near railway crossing Rahim Yar Khan

District Muzaffargarh

31/10/2010
Participants:
    Fazal e Rabb (Seraiki nationalist and activist)
    Muhammad Riaz
    Youth of Kot Adu
Place: Fazal e Rabb's home, behind main bazaar, District Kot Adu, Muzaffargarh

01/11/2010
Participants:
    Muhammad Akram Chandio Baloch (School teacher and activist)
    Muhammad Younas (Farmer, victim of army allotment)
    A patwari and some local youth of the town
Place: Muslim League Office, Chowk Munda, Tehsil Kot Adu, District Muzaffargarh

District Layyah

01/11/2010
Participants:
    Malik Afzal Jagwal (Lawyer, land owner)
    Lawyers from Chaubara and a medical doctor
Place: Basic Health Unit Chowk Azam District Layyah

District Khushab

03/03/2011
Participants:
    Sajad Haidar (Educationist)
    Lecturers and staff of Government Degree College Johar Abad
Place: Government Degree College Johar Abad

Appendix 3.4. State land put at the disposal of GHQ by the board of Revenue, Government of Punjab, for personal allocation under the Army Welfare Scheme, 1990–2010

District	Acres
Okara	43,466
Bahawalpur	11,117
Khanewal	45,119
Total	99,702

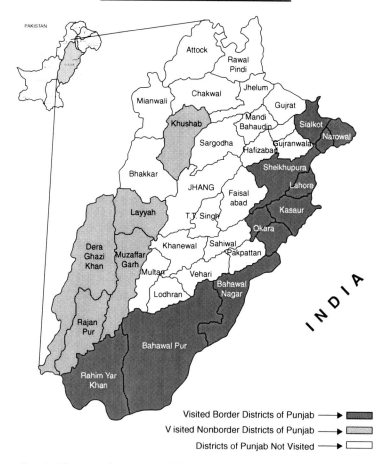

Visited Border Districts of Punjab ⟶ ▓
Visited Nonborder Districts of Punjab ⟶ ▒
Districts of Punjab Not Visited ⟶ ☐

Source: Board of Revenue, Government of Punjab.

Appendix 3.5

A. Area leased out to the army

No.	Name of place	Area	Year of lease
1	KPT Range	98,755 acres	1978
2	Din Gargh Range	85,000 acres	1978
3	Near Qasim Wala Bangla	602 acres 2 kanals	1981
4	Chak No. 320/HR	24 acres	1988
5	Chak No. 252/HL	14 acres 3 kanals 12 marlas	1988
6	Adjacent to Dahar Ganwar Wali	225 acres	1989
7	Near Chak No. 268/HL	9 acres	1990
8	Near Chak No. 165/Murad	187 acres 4 kanals	1997
9	Adjacent to Chak No. 23 & 27/BC	2,600 acres	2007
10	Surian Cantt	20,575 acres	2010
	Total	**207,992 acres 1 Kanal 13 Marlas**	

B. Area purchased by the army

1. New Cantt   8,500 acres
2. Adjacent to Chak No. 273 & 278/HR   103 acres
3. Asrani Bridge   55 acres 1 Kanal 13 Marlas

Total: 8,708 acres 1 Kanal 13 Marals

C. Area subletted out or leased out to the army

1. KPT Range   800 acres
2. Asrani Bridge   55 acres
3. Adjacent to Chak No. 23 & 27/BC   2,000 acres

Total: 2,855 acres

D. Area in illegal possession of the army

1. Adjacent to KPT Maneuvering area   600 acres
2. Feroza Range (Area demanded but no leased out so far)   85,945 acres
3. Dahar Chapli   3,700 acres
4. Asrani Bridge   113 acres
5. Chak No. 68/DB (Area demanded but none leased out so far)   70 acres

6. Adjacent to Wahni

Chak No. 54/DNB	912 acres
Chak No. 55/DNB	1,775 acres
Chak No. 56/DNB	1,800 acres
Chak No. 62/DNB	1,400 acres
Chak No. 63/DNB	175 acres
Chak No. 65/DNB	1,625 acres
Chak No. 66/DNB	1,525 acres
Chak No. 73/DNB	225 acres
(Area demanded but none leased out so far)	9,437 acres
	Total: 99,865 acres

E. Area leased illegally by the army

1. Adjacent to KPT maneuvering area	600 acres
2. Feroza Range	11,000 acres
3. Dahar Chapli	3,700 acres
4. Asrani Bridge	113 acres
5. Basti Wahni	1,250 acres
6. Toba Badwani	400 acres
	Total: 17,063 acres

Notes

1 For example, in the army, the hierarchy is soldier, or *sepoy*, lance *naik*, noncommissioned officers (NCOs), including *naik, havaldar*, junior commissioned officers (JCO), including *naib sobedar, sobedar (jamadar* in the Armored Corps) and *sobedar* major. It is possible to rise through the ranks and reach officer status. This includes honorary lieutenant and captain ranks. The officer hierarchy for those who pass out of the Pakistan Military Academy in Kakul, Abbottabad, is second lieutenant, lieutenant, captain, major, lieutenant colonel, colonel, brigadier (one star), major general, lieutenant general, full general (four star) and field marshall.

2 *Patwar halqa* depends on population and size of the union council.

3 There appears to be a historic precedent for such border allocations ranging back to Athen's conflict with Sparta. For details, refer to Mitchell (2000). Thanks to Zulqarnain Dogar for pointing this out to us.

4 One *marla* is 30.25 square feet.

5 Our understanding of nonborder allotments is that the same basic rules of thumb apply.

6 The local government field hierarchy under the EDOR is district officer of revenue (DOR), deputy district officer of revenue (DDOR), Tehsildar, Naib Tehsildar, Qanon Go and, most critically, the *patwari*, who registers the land and maintains the record. The *patwari* possess immense power despite being on the lowest rung of this hierarchy. It is common knowledge across Pakistani society that *patwaris* take great liberty in manipulating land transactions.

7 Indeed, in some cases, lands being allotted to military personnel do not fall into the category of agricultural land. For example, right alongside GT Road near Pirowal in

Khanewal district, approximately 8000 acres of land in the possession of the Punjab Forest Department has recently been handed over to GHQ.

8 Intriguingly, in some cases these newer conflicts have led to considerable reordering of earlier political alignments. For example, tensions between Urdu-speaking settlers and the local Siraiki population have persisted for a number of decades since partition. However, Urdu speakers have tended more recently to ally themselves with Siraikis in opposition to newer Punjabi settlers. The Muttahida Qaumi Movement (MQM) has recognized this shift and been a vocal supporter of the Siraiki province demand.

9 All of this information was obtained from the personal record of Dr. Ayesha Siddiqa, whom we wish to acknowledge.

10 A few names are made up because some individuals expressed the desire to remain anonymous.

References

Mitchell, K. 2000. "Land Allocation and Self-Sufficiency in the Ancient Athenian Village." *Agricultural History* 74 (1), 1–18.

Siddiqa, A. 2007. *Military Inc.: Inside Pakistan's Military Economy*. Karachi: Oxford University Press.

Chapter Four

THE MILITARY'S AGRARIAN LAND ACQUISITIONS: HIGH HANDEDNESS AND SOCIAL RESENTMENT

Introduction

As explained in chapter 3, the military's agrarian land acquisitions in the postcolonial period were initially concentrated in the border regions. However, it has been in nonborder districts that the more recent and intensive land allotments have taken place. In this chapter we provide details of our research in these new allotment areas. In short, we show that the historic policy of land allotment continues in nonborder zones, whereas there is little land left to allocate in the border zones.

We start, however, by documenting the multifarious activities of the Pakistan Rangers, a paramilitary force subject to military command, in the border districts. The fieldwork testimonies below provide a snapshot of the Rangers' dominant and intrusive role in the border regions. In each case, we highlight the daily experiences of local communities as impacted by the interaction with the Rangers. There is an amazing amount of similarity and consistency in the narratives across the border region.

For the best part of Pakistan's history, the military's purported role as heroic guardian of the state has gone largely unchallenged, within the Punjab at least. One of our objectives in this book is to provide a voice to those segments of Punjabi society that suffer the brunt of the military's voracious resource grabbing. It is this side of the story that needs to be told. We hope that other researchers will follow up on our exploratory findings by returning to the various locations listed in appendix 3.1.

Following the account of the Rangers' activities is a section on the limited allocations of land in border districts. Since most local informants talked at length about their perceptions of conditions across the border, we have devoted a section to that. We end the chapter with an account of nonborder allocations.

Rangers: Masters of Their Domain

The Rangers are the guardians of a five-mile belt along the border from Sialkot to Rahim Yar Khan. Their jurisdiction extends to policing the border to ensure there are no illegal crossings, infiltration of "enemy" agents or smuggling activities. In practice, we found that the police defers to them and accept as truth any allegation made by the Rangers. When a power struggle ensues, the police generally stand down. In practice, as is explained below, Rangers also often claim jurisdiction on activities of other ministries such as irrigation (to police waters) and forestry (to police forests and game).

The Rangers personnel with whom ordinary people come into direct contact in any particular border zone rarely include high-ranking officers. It may therefore be assumed that the subalterns and junior officers with whom ordinary villagers come into contact with are engaged in self-aggrandizement without the knowledge of their senior officers. We observed, for example, in every one of our research sites spread across all border districts, that low-ranking Rangers personnel at checkpoints set up within a five-mile radius of the border routinely stopped and harassed villagers going to and from their villages. A standard operating procedure of sorts has been adopted whereby eggs, milk, vegetables and other such goods are given over to Rangers at check posts as a small bribe, so as to be spared serious extortion. Vehicles (including cycles) are commandeered, chores demanded and tractors made to work on Rangers' projects. If Rangers buy something from a local shop, they do so on credit, which is rarely honored.[1]

In Tehsil Bahawalnagar, overweight vehicles are allowed to cross the bridge at Head Suleman Ki for a bribe. Farmers who cultivate next to the border have to get tokens as permission and these can be denied if services are not rendered to those issuing the tokens.[2] The cattle of noncooperative farmers are denied access to drinking water from the *awami* (peoples) canal. In Tehsil Sialkot, Rs100 per trolley is charged by the Rangers as a tax if a farmer needs mud or sand from a *nullah's* (Hec and Dec) flood-season banks to level his land or for construction. In village Meerowal, District Sheikhupura, Rangers sell sand for Rs 400 per tractor trolley. This is even charged from farmers who are taking mud from their own land. In Tehsil Shakargarh of District Narowal, provision of a mobile calling card to Rangers personnel at check posts is the main currency to avoiding harassment. *Begar* (forced) labor and asking for chores from those who possess vehicles, tractors, trolleys,or loaders is routine.[3]

The following example perhaps sums up the general trend: very near the border in Tehsil Kasur of the same district, between the villages of Bhoki Ala and Sahjra kalan, is a Rangers' check post (built on privately owned land, as is generally the case) which is widely known throughout the area as the *talwar* (sword) check post. Over time, the local community has developed an alternative name for the check post: *mussibat* (trouble) post, because no one is allowed to transport crops, milk or any other good without giving a share to the Rangers personnel stationed at the post. Moreover, the *mussibat* extends to public transporters: the Rangers operate as *samosa* and *pakora* vendors and guarantee themselves a clientele because all public-transport drivers are required to treat the check post as a bus stop.[1] The villages in the locality of the check post harvest *arvi* (local vegetable) in May and June, and in that period many trucks are loaded from the fields and sent to different parts of the country. The Rangers collect commission from every truck that passes the check post.

If the Rangers' rent-seeking was limited to such petty activities, it would be impossible to distinguish them from ordinary police who routinely harass, intimidate and extort ordinary people at check posts throughout the country. Indeed, the Rangers also appear to ape the police in many districts where they act as mediators in the case of personal disputes, for which they take bribes.[5] The actions by both forces are subject to reproach but our concern here is with the Rangers who are under military command.

As we suggested in chapter 1, we found that the Rangers have developed a business structure at the local level in border zones that is a microcosm of the corporate empire of the military. In short, Rangers' activities are systematic and not limited to only a few errant individuals. Both institutions benefit at the expense of the general population and both crowd out private sector activity. At the macro level, explicit, though nontransparent, subsidies benefit the military. At the micro level, the Rangers depend on implicit subsidies, extortion and drawing the resources of other government departments for personal benefit.

There are a number of enterprises that Rangers personnel – and the scale and uniformity of the enterprises suggests the involvement of high-ranking officials – have established and run throughout the border districts. Some of these enterprises suggest a significant level of urbanization in areas where remote and previously low-value lands have been transformed into suburban real estate. While similar to the cantonment-based model of development, Rangers' complexes represent new trends that reflect the imperatives of a much more complex division of labor in a society characterized by increasingly differentiated sources of wealth.

Via delegation or otherwise, Rangers have commoditized natural resources including water bodies, forests and wildlife. Aside from the obvious private gains garnered by the Rangers through this process, it is inappropriate that civilian authorities that are tasked with the public responsibility of managing these commons have been displaced.

One of the practices of the Rangers is to regulate local communities' trimming or cutting of trees on their own property. The border guardians claim that trees must be protected because they provide shade for soldiers and camouflage during hostilities. Thus, tree cutting requires military authorization in the border zone.[6] However, the Rangers' implementation of this restriction demonstrates the flagrant abuse of power that takes place at the grassroots level.

In Tehsil Bahawalnagar, farmers are not allowed to cut trees, or even branches above a diameter of nine inches, anywhere in the five-mile border zone. This extends to trees in farmers' courtyards, and permission even has to be sought for cutting dead trees. The Rangers, we were told, have made a deal with *pathan* contractors from outside the area for the tree cutting at much below market rates. Farmers have stopped planting trees and the area looks completely denuded. The Rangers subsequently announced a tree plantation drive which was a failure since trees initially need intensive care to mature and local communities have no incentive to support such projects.

In Tehsil Fort Abbas of the same district, farmers have also stopped tree-planting because of the permit needed for harvesting. A rich border forest referred to as Dodhla has been virtually denuded, and it is commonly understood that the Rangers permit cutting for a stipulated fee. A local *numberdar* (village headman) secured a permit, after having to travel 600 kilometers to Okara (district headquarters), to have some trees cut on his land. Even though he had a permit, the Rangers insisted on a commission of Rs10,000 for the cutting.

In Sialkot and Sheikhupura, the lack of trees is again evident in the border zone, and farmers claim that they are not even allowed to touch windfall trees. The transactions costs of gaining permission for cutting for household needs are so high that the farmers have simply decided not to plant. Here again the double standards are evident: Rangers are openly contracting out tree cutting on state lands.

In Tehsil Shakargarh of District Narowal, Rangers contract out the cutting of trees on state lands or lands not claimed by allottees. On such land, and even on land left fallow by locals, the Rangers lay claim to all wild growth. This includes *kana* (a form of local bamboo), *kaai* (used to make a kind of rope, paper, and cardboard) and *khar* (used for making *jharus*: a local broom for sweeping). In Rahim Yar Khan, the southernmost border district, Rangers routinely chop down trees for their furniture requirements from the bank of canal Patan Manara minor that passes near the village 101p Luckiwala. Even the trees in the neighboring Cotton Research Farm are not spared.[7]

A similar logic applies to fishing and wildlife. Rangers have taken over the guardianship of fisheries and effectively control all fishing contracts. In Bahawalnagar, they have displaced the local fish-stalls selling fish kebobs to bus passengers and have hired their own vendors as wage labor. In Sialkot, local communities are prohibited by the Rangers from catching fish during flood season, even if the *nallah* (rivulet) passes through their property. In the village of Raji Ala in Kasur, the Rangers have established a fish farm (another common activity), and according to local informants they have never paid for electricity because they do not have a legal WAPDA connection. This practice of not paying electric bills is widespread throughout the border zone.[8]

In Bahawalnagar, Sialkot and Sheikhpura, hunting for, or contracting out, wild game like partridges, ducks, quails and wild beast is exclusively the Rangers' prerogative. In Rahim Yar Khan, Rangers have developed a virtual monopoly on hunting activities. The wide expanse of desert in which the border zone is located can only be traversed with Rangers' vehicles, and the few nomadic populations that wandered the area and hunted deer and tilor (migratory game bird) have been almost completely deprived of their historic livelihoods. Rangers manage hunting parties whenever a high-ranking official visits the area, and also facilitate their own designated hunting networks. Those who do not enjoy the good graces of the Rangers have to pay huge bribes if they want to engage in what is formally an illegal activity.[9] Meanwhile, residents of the village Rampura, District Lahore, resentfully told us that they could not even kill wild boars that destroy their crops.

Rahim Yar Khan has also become a home away from home for rich Arab sheiks. They routinely spend the winter months in the area and are given virtual state-protocol by the Rangers; the latter serve as the sheiks' hunting guides and also facilitate other leisure activities. The Arabs have taken huge chunks of land from the government on lease and there is no restriction on their hunting of deer and tilor.[10]

Another major commercial enterprise is the use of state land to build and rent out marriage halls, shopping plazas and playgrounds. The shops are rented out and fees charged for the use of playgrounds. In Tehsil Shakargarh, District Narowal, the Rangers charge Rs10,000 per marriage on a lawn that they have recently opened for public use. The lighting rented for the opening ceremony has yet to be paid for. When building a rangers' shopping corner in the main market, a neighboring shop was taken over and inventory thrown out. Even the judgment of the High Court in favor of the property owner has not persuaded the Rangers to restore possession to the rightful owner. Instead, locals pointed to a fully armed ranger standing guard outside the shops that have been leased for rent. More generally, we found that all state land that is currently unoccupied or unclaimed has been taken over by Rangers for use without any legal mandate, and windfall rents are accrued by them.

Commercial activities are not confined to the border area either. Rangers in Rahim Yar Khan have established a Rohi Mart in the middle of the city, a western-type superstore, which is the biggest and most modern store in the city. Rangers run this store. The bottles of soft drinks are refilled illegally by a Rangers' factory in Chak No. 4 and are available at the railway station of the city and other city locations.

The Rangers have also set up schools in most of the border zones. In Kasur, Rangers' schools advertise an Oxford syllabus, although the quality of the teaching is said to be poor. While children of ranger families attend for free, others have to pay full fee. In Bahawalnagar, Rangers launched a fund-raising drive to open a high school that would be open to the public. Local families who contributed were resentful that their children were subsidizing the children of Rangers' families with their much higher tuition fees. In Tehsil Fort Abbas, a high school built on Cholistan Development Authority land is viewed as the best in the city and children of Rangers' families are subsidized while other children pay full fee. In Sialkot, a Rangers' school on private occupied land provides subsidized education to Rangers' families and full fee education to others who can afford it. The school was entirely built with *begar* (forced labor) and forced donations such as bricks from the nearby kiln. Artisans were rounded up and not paid and others were forced to contribute material.

Perhaps the most brazen Rangers business that we found in several border districts involved the manufacturing and marketing of a cola-like soda, which, at least temporarily, displaced Pepsi in the local market. Bonafide Pepsi producers have been forced to shut down their operations, and Rangers use empty Pepsi bottles to market their own alternative. In Bahawalnagar, Pepsi retaliated by undercutting the Rangers' soda price, which forced the latter to close its bottling plant. The Rangers subsequently established a chiller and milk was bought from local farmers at below market rates and sold on to companies like Nestle and Haleeb. Nestle protested the lack of direct access to farmers; the chiller also failed as an enterprise. In Shakargarh, the fake Pepsi business had been shut down by an effective campaign launched by a Pepsi representative. Other ventures have also had variable success – but the point is that the Rangers continue to take on commercial ventures which result in a diversion of public monies, crowd out of private sector activities and violate human rights.[11]

Natural resources and commercial enterprises are not all that the Rangers lay claim to. We were told during fieldwork that Rangers often occupy the rest houses of government departments (a perk for senior bureaucrats and their families in scenic remote areas where other facilities are not available). For example, in the village Sarja Mirja, District Lahore, the Irrigation Department's rest house has been taken over. Occupying private land for commercial ventures and schools was commonplace in Jhata Putha, a small town in Tehsil Khanpur, District Rahim Yar Khan; they encroached on property belonging to the Ministry of Agriculture, including buildings and a date farm.

In general, we were informed that complaints to senior military officers for redress against high-handed behavior came to nothing. In some cases, when villages brave a reprisal and get the ear of a good and sympathetic senior officer, the offending party is transferred. As inhabitants of the village Rampura, District Lahore, told us, such cases of redress are an exception to the rule.

The Punjab Rangers have gained notoriety for engaging in resource-grabbing activities that represent transgression not only of their formal mandate, but also of the public interest at large. As a border force, the Rangers operate throughout Pakistan, and over the past many years there have been numerous accounts of abuse of power by Rangers in other provinces, particularly in Sindh.

First, Rangers have played a significant role in the political and economic life of Karachi for the best part of two decades. While the biggest complaint against Rangers, routinely leveled by a wide cross section of the city's population, is that of excessive use of force in the name of law and order, plenty of anecdotes have emerged over the years to suggest that the Rangers have been party to the endemic practice of land-grabbing that has almost become a defining feature of life in Karachi.[12] While the Rangers may not be the only state institution involved in the pillaging of Karachi's resources, it is one of the more prominent and powerful ones.

Second, directly correlated to the systematic corporate activities of the Punjab Rangers is the Sindh Rangers' involvement in an insidious subcontracting racket in the fishing sector. The Rangers' activities have come to light over the past few years due to the quite dramatic emergence of a people's movement of indigenous fishing communities in the coastal regions of Badin and Thatta.[13]

In short, water bodies that have historically functioned as common property have, over the past couple of decades, been systematically identified by Rangers' as lucrative sources of income and commoditized accordingly. This means that Rangers have decreed themselves arbiters in all matters related to the catching and marketing of fish, forcing local fisher folk to sell their catch to Rangers' preferred subcontractors at artificially depressed rates. Arrangements are subsequently made by the Rangers' subcontractor to transport the fish from the water body in question to the designated fish market – which in the case of Badin and Thatta is typically Karachi – where sales to wholesalers and retailers guarantees windfall profits. The crucial feature of this whole racket is, as in the case of Punjab, that it takes place in and around the border zone.

The coasts of Badin and Thatta are very remote; the isolation enabled the Rangers to continue with their extortion for many years before the practices became common knowledge.

While we did not conduct any of our formal fieldwork for this book in Sindh, one of the authors has spent some time at the southern-most tip of District Badin where fishing communities head out to the Arabian Sea. Getting to Zero Point, the intersection of Pakistani and Indian coastal waters, entails driving through a dirt road off the main thoroughfare for at least 10 kilometres. The only presence on this road is the Sindh Rangers, who have set up check posts every 2 to 3 kilometers under the guise of security. However, it became clear during trips to Zero Point that the Rangers were more concerned with regulating the transport of fish, and strangers who were not privy to their commercial enterprise were not welcome.

Successive governments since the 1970s have also formally contracted out rights to marine resources across Sindh (and other provinces as well), which has had an extremely deleterious effect on the livelihoods of indigenous fishing communities. However, in the Rangers' case, the practice is completely without any formal mandate and is associated with extreme levels of exploitation and abuse of power.

We mention this example to highlight that the corporate interests of the Pakistan Rangers are limited not only to Punjab, but extend, in all likelihood, to all parts of the country. There can be little doubt that resistance to this systematic extortion may bring together historically estranged nationalities in Pakistan with ordinary people in Punjab.

Border-Land Allocations

Military land allotments in border zones now constitute a small proportion of the overall military land acquisitions. As pointed out in chapter 3, a large number of the original allottees in the Border Allocation Scheme sold out very soon after they were given rights to the land. There are some cases where individual military men have systematically acquired large amounts of land in a particular border zone. However, military allottees are now relatively few and far between.

In the field, we mostly heard of disastrous allocations for NCOs (see chapter 3), particularly those being rewarded for serving valiantly in the Kargil conflict (1999) with India in Kashmir. The decorations came with land allocations, sometimes posthumously. We learned in the field that many of these allocations were barren uncultivable tracts that were so far from where the soldiers' and NCOs' families reside that they were never even visited. In such cases, the allocations were viewed merely as a formality.

The bulk of NCOs that had claimed their allocations have sold and left, very much like their senior officers. Via contacts in Kasur, we were able to question some *patwaris*, who maintain land records, including allocations to the military, about how much total land is in their *halqa* (jurisdiction), how much of that is allocated to the military and how much is still retained by the military. It appears that most of the officers have indeed sold their lands or are renting them out. In any case, allottees are not personally managing the farms as the border scheme intended.

In one case, a brigadier who made a sale later reclaimed the land. The purchaser took the case to the Lahore High Court and won the case, but the Border Committee argued that the petitioner needed to produce a NOC issued by GHQ for the year the sale was made. The brigadier was able to reclaim the land. While the legal position has been explained in chapter 3, this case suggests that there are exceptions based on the amount of leverage that can be exercised by someone with connections. In other cases, we were told at the Revenue Department in Lahore that military officers who had successfully sold land subsequently petitioned the military for more land, claiming that they had none at the time of retirement.

In Bahawalnagar, we ascertained that only three military men had settled on the border land. One was a brigadier who had been buying from other military men and expanding his holdings. The other was a colonel and the third was a NCO. The brigadier was alleged to have used soldiers for farm work when he was in service. The ground water was brackish and canal water was scarce. One of the complaints by local farmers against the brigadier was water theft, which reduced the former's share.[11] A formal complaint was launched by a farmer to the irrigation department to no avail.

Two group discussions with famers revealed that military officers renting out land merely show up to collect their rent, and in this regard they are no different from other landlords. However, since military men have direct access to district and subdistrict revenue officials, they are able to solve land-related problems much more easily than the local farmers. The farmers unanimously view the border allocation scheme to have been a failure since the military men did not stay on as they were supposed to and it was "the sweat of the local farmers" that ensured the development of the local land. The growing sense of injustice is compounded by the high-handed behavior of the Rangers. Our impression is that farmers were initially willing to respect state allocated property rights, but that retrospectively the grievances inflicted on them resulted in questioning the injustice of these allocations.

In the village of Ghowind in District Lahore, 2,700 acres, of 3,600 acres of arable land, was allotted to ex-army men – but only a few have retained ownership of this land. In an adjacent village Rampura, old allotments have been overshadowed by a recent land-appropriation episode. After the Kargil conflict in 1999, the army built a 20 km long defense bund (wall) stretching from the Wahga border to Ghowind village. At some places, the bund is 20 feet high. The army promised compensation to farmers whose land was used for this defense purpose, but those affected in Rampura are still waiting for the promised compensation.

In Sialkot, farmers complained that they were being made to build defense bunds (mud defense walls) on this side of the border, as well as *morchas* (bunkers), using their own tractors and diesel. The farmers have received no compensation for the work, expense or even for the land so acquired, sometimes up to four canals of private property.[15] When the villagers resisted, the running of tube wells to irrigate the fields was blocked, with Rangers claiming that the noise of the engine disturbed them. As always, the villagers eventually complied. Since troublemakers can be picked up on false charges for being Indian spies or smugglers, villagers are intimidated into accepting demands. Similarly, in Kasur a mud wall has been constructed along the border. The villages informed us that legally only 10 feet of land is required but the Rangers appropriated 40 feet and the affected villagers have still not been compensated.

In Rahim Yar Khan, a new cantonment is under construction at Chowk Bahadur. Local smallholders have been forced to sell their land to the army at artificially low prices. Meanwhile, a reported 85,000 acres has been recently allotted at Qasim Bella. Near Khanpur more than 1,000 acres of land on both sides of the Aab e Hayat canal was allotted to retired army men at a reported rates of Rs340 per acre (ridiculously below market prices); much of this land has been rented out to nonlocals. The impression we got was that there is some form of military land allotment in every small town or village in Rahim Yar Khan – if local communities resist the allotments, force is employed.

On the Other Side

An intriguing contrast was evident throughout the border districts in terms of how land is used and maintained. A number of local people insisted that we observe the differences between the Pakistani and Indian sides of the border. In Bahawalnagar, we were allowed to climb the 60 foot observation tower at Zero Point and use the binoculars kept up there for observation. It truly was a stark contrast. It was almost as if one were looking from the West Bank or Gaza onto a fertile Israeli kibbutz. We stared from denuded landscape onto a lush and wooded one. The Indian observation post seemed large and cushy compared to the spartan quarters we were looking out from. Even the Indian observation tower was much higher at 150 feet. The roads were paved, while we had gotten stuck in the sand three times on our way to and from the check post on the dirt road. We saw plenty of tube wells and tractors and other farm machinery, suggesting a high level of mechanization. Perhaps water makes all the difference or perhaps it is because the agriculture is owner operated – as opposed to the absentee farming practiced by the Pakistani military.

Local farmers claim that their counterparts on the Indian side of the border have plenty of irrigation water, tube wells, roads and electricity, and the result is an agriculture that looks noticeably superior. They also point out that Indian soldiers are willing to work for the cotton stalks that they need for fuel, whereas on this side of the border, the Rangers imperiously demand it. In Bahawalpur, we were again told that electricity, roads and water accounted for productive agriculture on the other side of the border. We were unable to confirm this for ourselves since the paved road stopped about 80 km short of the border and we could not afford the two four-wheel-drive vehicles recommended for the journey. In Narowal, we were told that by the time they sow, Indian wheat is already six inches tall. Subsidized electricity, water, credit, fertilizer and other inputs is said to be the reason. In Sialkot, we heard yet again that land across the border was wooded, and modern mechanized agriculture was being practiced with many state facilities, which included subsidized access to canal water, credit, electricity and the construction of roads and embankments as needed.

Pakistani farmers claim that the Indian side is always responsible for the clearance of mines, while they suffer numerous accidents after border tensions; some informants said that after the 1971 war they came back to find that their houses had been raided by the so-called caretakers. In Tehsil Fort Abbas of District Bahawalnagar a *numberdar* was resentful that in previous face offs with the Indian military, the border was mined and all farmers removed from the border area. Many farmers, including the *numberdar*, lost standing crops and were promised compensation. He claimed that many have been compensated several times over, but he has yet to receive his compensation. The demining was incomplete and here also, as in other places, there were several injuries to animals, though there was no loss of life.

It is more than likely that the constructed dichotomy of the Pakistani military as oppressive and self-interested and the Indian military as responsible and selfless is, at best, a half-truth. But it is important to reiterate again that we had not thought of engaging in a comparison – to the extent that one is possible – prior to heading into the field. Local informants in almost all districts insisted that we at least gather anecdotes that, for our informants, prove that our guardians are not nearly as noble as those outside the border zones often believe.

Nonborder Allocations

This section reinforces the central point made above regarding the abuse of authority – in this case by senior military officers. By contrast, the treatment meted out to subaltern ranks is shoddy. In District Bahawalnagar, Tehsil Bahawalnagar, we learned that land granted to the soldiers, NCOs and JCOs is often not worth having as it was dispersed in bits and pieces all over the place. Alternatively, they are often allocated land in places where there is no water. Senior officers are more likely to get consolidated land and in places where there is access to water.

The process of allotments in Cholistan (Bhawalnagar, Bahawalpur and Rahim Yar Khan) works in the same way as explained in chapter 3, but the implementation is via the Cholistan Development Authority (CDA) and is particularly illustrative of our point. The last four managing directors of CDA have been military men (four major generals and one brigadier). This has greatly facilitated the process of land allocations to the military and made public protest ineffectual.

These allotments have been to senior, serving and retired, officers. For example, General Musharraf acquired two squares while in office. No taxes were paid and there are implicit subsidies in land development such as the use of government machinery and soldiers for private use. CDA officials informed us of cases were land allocated for military use, such as firing ranges, were converted into personal allocations. In many cases, existing tenants were evicted. As in other districts, most have sold land or rented it, while a few have not bothered to show up to make a claim. We learned in a lawyer group discussion that the Indian Army also makes land allocations to retired military officials across the border in Rajastan, but that it is 25 acres irrespective of rank. Unlike the practice of the Pakistani military, which discourages domicile allocations, the Indian allotments are to original residents of the area.

We saw farms belonging to ex-generals, including General Musharraf, and the amount of investment that has gone into developing them. Driving to General Musharraf's farm was a revelation. From a barely drivable metal road, there is suddenly a high-quality (though still narrow) paved road leading to the farm. The channels are also beautifully paved and water is drawn from a distribution canal two kilometers away. A pond filled with water is used to pump water to fields that the channels are not able to serve at a higher elevation. Cotton crops are lined by heavily-laden date palms. We were told that serving soldiers and government machinery had been used to level and develop the land. We were also told that in the development of land belonging to senior military officers, sand had been dumped on neighboring fields that belonged to NCOs and JCOs making their development task harder.[16]

In one case, a senior military officer was not able to get irrigation water from a local distribution channel leading away from a canal because his land was at a higher elevation. His response was to have the distribution channel elevated by the irrigation department. The consequence is that water is now only available in the distribution channel when the canal water level is high.

When the water level is low, all the local farmers who have legal *khuls* (outlets) on the distribution channel are denied water. Prior to the elevation of the distribution channel they got some water even when the water level in the irrigation channel was low.

We were told that rural development funds coming to Cholistan were also appropriated by the retired military officers with land allotments. Thus, a large water course paving scheme approved by the Asian Development Bank was diverted to improving channels on land allocated to senior military officers. This is also alleged to be the case for water course improvement done by the largest government established NGO, the National Rural Support Program, which has a mandate to alleviate poverty.

In Tehsil Fort Abbas, District Bahawalnagar, there is wide-spread resentment of the extensive military allocations, though most local people feel that no one can afford to raise this issue at any forum. Particularly grating is the alleged allocation of land to General Musharraf's domestic staff members (sweeper and gardener) in village 224/-9r. Much of the land allotted to the lower ranks in the military remained unclaimed due to the lack of water. We were told that General Musharraf's initial allocation was also in this area, but that he managed a relocation to Tehsil Bahalwalpur (the village of Sheikhoshijra) which has canal water access.

In Rajanpur, the Air Force has appropriated land on the outskirts of the city near union council Fatehpur. State land (335 acres) in the form of a *rakh* (common property), utilized by the local communities for decades, was forcibly acquired in 2001–2002. This land is adjacent to the Fareed Air Base. Local people talk of a continuous expansion of the Base's boundaries. There has been no attempt to provide legal cover to this expansion and it is therefore impossible to know exactly how this land has been subdivided. Some local farmers have rented squares from high-ranking officers who have come to serve at Fareed Air Base. It is an open secret in the area that the land is serviced by water routinely stolen from the Fatehpur minor canal.

Ranger officials have extended land appropriation to Rajanpur as well, even though it is one of the western-most districts of Punjab and therefore far removed from the Indian border. In the village *Kotla Pehlwan* in Tehsil Rajanpur, 150 acres of *rakh* land was occupied by the Rangers in 2007. Local farmers were evicted from the lands under the pretext that a training school was being established there. Instead, the Rangers proceeded to cultivate the lands until May 2010, when the civilian government temporarily ended the Rangers' occupation. However, a few months later a retired major reoccupied the land armed with a court order which reflected the subordination of the judiciary to the military. As with the lands occupied by the Air Force, in this case too water was stolen from a nearby *Hazooriwa* canal.

During our time in Rajanpur, we were also informed that 500 acres in the so-called Dhundi Estate was allotted to army officials, whereas in Tehsil Rojhan a total of 3,500 acres has been made available to all three of the armed forces personnel. In District Muzaffargarh, more than 50 thousand acres of state land is allotted to different ranking officers of the military. Much of this land is formally designated as barren, whereas in fact it has been under the cultivation of local farmers since the colonial period. These farmers have consistently been paying taxes (*tirini*) to the government. The two most substantial allottee areas are Rakh Azizabad and Rakh Sadiqabad, which account for a total of 30,000 acres of the total allotted land. Both serving and retired military personnel are beneficiaries. The pattern of allotment is nothing less than draconian. Local communities who have been cultivating these *rakhs* only find out about the military allottees when eviction crews arrive to drive the farmers off the land. As earlier indicated, it is rarely the case the allottees work the land on their own – in some cases they bring wage laborers with them and in others desperate local farmers who have been disenfranchised end up offering their labor to the new owners.

The pattern of the allotment in Layyah is also tilted toward military officers who act as absentee landlords. In Tehsil Chobara near the town Nawakot, 820 squares (20,500 acres) of the Rakh Kona were allotted to officers and NCOs in 1982–83. The price of the land was a nominal Rs146 per acre, payable over 20 years. As in other regions, it appears that the lands allotted to senior officers are of far higher quality than those allotted to NCOs; the former also have access to water. In Rakh Jaded in the same *tehsil*, 40 square (1,000 acres) have also been allotted along the same pattern.

Summary and Conclusions

While our original intension was to explore the state of military allocations on the border and its comparative productivity, our field research soon showed that the big story on the border is the high-handed behavior of the Pakistan Rangers, a paramilitary force subject to military command. They act like sovereigns and treat the commons and state resources, including fisheries, forests and game, as their own. They also oppress local communities to expand their business. They establish social sector facilities like schools for their own use with forced local contributions, and local access is subsequently based on a fee. All of these for-profit businesses represent a microcosm of the military ventures on a macro level and they forcibly displace or otherwise crowd out private sector activities.

Such is the resentment of local communities that this may color their perception of conditions across the border. They view the conditions across the border as much better due to robust agriculture benefiting from state support in terms of credit, inputs and infrastructure. They also perceive the Rangers across the border to be courteous rather than predatory based on stories heard form those with relatives across the border. Casual observation certainly seems to suggest much more lush conditions prevailing across the border in contrast to the deforested and denuded conditions on the Pakistani side. The military certainly is losing the public relations battle for hearts and minds.

The nonborder allocations also represent a case study in privilege and abuse of office. Senior military officers have been allocated prime land, have access to irrigation facilities and use state resources to develop their land, including serving soldiers. NCO lands are of poor quality and in many cases the allotments are simply a formality. It is worth exploring this point in more detail because the extent to which the Pakistani military is a cohesive force is an important question, and the issue of material benefits accruing to different ranks could be a crucial determinant in this regard. We have already documented that the history of land allotments – at least in the postcolonial period – has evolved such that NCOs and JCOs have become increasingly marginalized, both in terms of the quality of the allotments made and the quantity of such allotments, whereas the senior officer corps is now more and more in the habit of adding to already significant hauls of state land.[17]

At the same time, it is important to bear in mind that the lower ranks of the Pakistani military nevertheless do continue to enjoy a relatively exalted status in society at large. Not only do they benefit from welfare schemes – of which land allotments are only one type – their association with the country's most powerful institution holds them in good stead in society more generally. Perhaps as significant as any other factor in explaining the relative lack of discontent within the forces is the security that employment within the military brings with it, which is becoming arguably more important with the relative decline of agriculture and limited livelihood opportunities in urban areas. The military, too, has made a conscious attempt to expand the bases of new recruitment into the office corps so that relatively underrepresented ethnic groups are co-opted into the biggest collective welfare organization in Pakistan.[18]

Having said this, it is also true that some discontent within the forces does become common knowledge every so often. It could be that this discontent is related more to the military's political blunders, or strategic shifts such as those engendered by the alliance with NATO in the so-called war on terror. As far as material benefits are concerned, it appears as if the military continues to successfully placate its lower ranks.

In any case, as we have documented in this chapter, the fate of local communities is much worse than NCOs and JCOs. Households who have been relying on the public commons to meet their livelihood needs for decades have been unceremoniously evicted with the connivance of district administrations, including the police. It is the high-handed examples of abuse of power documented in this chapter that is engendering resentment and resistance of a qualitatively new kind. It is to these responses of violated local communities to which we turn next in chapter 5.

Notes

1 We found a comment of one local, regarding the way they have to deal with Rangers, particularly striking: "We have to kill our egos."
2 An example of a rendered service is providing tractors for land leveling as demanded by the Rangers.
3 Not even friends are spared. We were told a story of a young man who fraternized with the Rangers and made available his motorbike and DVD player for pornographic movies until there was a falling out and a physical fight ensued. The young man disappeared from the village but a group of armed Rangers kept hounding his family long after to reveal his whereabouts.
4 There are also numerous examples of the Rangers as a collective looking out for themselves at the expense of the local population. In Bahawalnagar, the Rangers had apparently appropriated the Irrigation Department's rest house for use as they deemed fit. We got stuck on the way to a border post because the bricks from the brick road had been systematically removed for barrack improvements in the Rangers' quarters. The patches where the bricks were missing forced us to move onto the sand tracks on the side of the road, which caused us to get stuck.
5 The police is, of course, empowered to formally mediate by using the law as an impartial mechanism to ensure justice is dispensed. In everyday Pakistan, the police invoke the law selectively and fleece individuals and parties embroiled in a conflict by threatening legal punishment that may or may not actually be called for in any particular case. While such abuse of power by police can be seen as an overstepping of its mandate, in the case of the Rangers no such mandate exists in the first place.
6 While tree-cutting restrictions represent military policy, villagers in Ghowind, a large village 2.5 kilometers away from the border in District Lahore, have to get approval for everything from the Rangers, including constructing a home. We were informed that countermanding arbitrary rules results in restrictions on plowing, or irrigating land, on the zero line (right next to the border). This is self-defeating as the Rangers claim a share from every irrigated field close to the border.
7 However, this was the only place where we found some measure of amity between the villagers and the Rangers. People living in the area provide milk, meat and almost anything the Rangers ask for, given their capacity, and in exchange the Rangers who have access to government vehicles that work in desert conditions cart materials for them as needed.
8 In the village 101p, Lakhiwala, the Water and Power Development Authority (WAPDA) officials cut the Ranger line for nonpayment of bills, but the Rangers reconnected illegally and blocked WAPDA personnel from coming near the premises of a building they had occupied.

9 In Shakargarh (Narowal), the Rangers allowed a local hunter five shots for Rs1,000 each – the hunter was told that he would have to cart off the big game kill, if there was one, on his own.

10 There has been the occasional news item which confirms that Arabs have been leased out public land in Rahim Yar Khan (for agriculture use as well as other pursuits) but we were not able to acquire any written documentation to this effect.

11 At the Ganda Singh border, the flag raising ceremony was enjoyed by citizens as an entertaining spectacle that was free and open to the public. We were told that the Rangers have now levied a 10 rupee fee to watch this ceremony. They also run shops to sell memorabilia and goods to visitors.

12 Arif Hasan's "The politics of ethnicity" in *DAWN*, 25 June 2010, represents a concise explanation of the political-economy bases of violence in the country's biggest city.

13 This movement was organized by the Pakistan Fisherfolk Forum and generated considerable support across a wide cross section of political forces and civil society. See www.pff.org.pk for details on the history and chronology of the fisherfolk struggle.

14 The brigadier had dug an illegal *morga* (outlet) under the official one so he had two channels serving his farm when it was his turn to draw water from the canal.

15 While there are variations across region, there are about eight canals to an acre.

16 In one interview, we were informed that one of the generals had managed to get 12.5 acres allocated to his driver via CDA. This practice may have been widespread; *The News International* reported on 15 July 2011 that the National Accountability Bureau (NAB) has initiated action to get back military lands illegally awarded to civilians in Dera Ismael Khan during General Musharraf's tenure. NAB is dependent on the ruling of the military GHQ on this matter and was still awaiting a response to the inquiry.

17 In so far as military land allotments are disaggregated by rank in the historical literature, our sense is that the British were keenly aware of the importance of keeping NCOs and JCOs (locals could not rise to higher ranks) pacified, and therefore loyal, through such allotments.

18 This effort appears to have had success in getting proportional representation in Bolochistan, but Sindh was still under-represented in new officer recruits relative to its population size in 2005. For details and caveats on the data see Fair and Nawaz (2011, 17).

Reference

Fair, C. C. and Nawaz, S. 2011. "The Changing Pakistan Army Officer Corps." *Journal of Strategic Studies*, 34 (1), 63–94.

Chapter Five

FROM SOCIAL RESENTMENT TO SOCIAL RESISTANCE

"Talking against the army is like talking against God."
(Resident of a village in Lahore District)

Introduction

It is uncommon to be confronted with popular media reports about military excess in Punjab, especially its rural areas. This is in contrast with the almost daily narration of police and administrative abuse, as well as the tedium of local courts. Every so often, an isolated incident does come to the fore, but it typically is viewed as an anomaly, at least amongst the urban public. This trend, however, appeared to change irrevocably during the Musharraf dictatorship. An argument can be made that the taboo of speaking out against military excess in Punjab was permanently undone by the high-profile conflict that erupted in Okara in 2000 between landless tenant farmers and the administration of the so-called Okara military farms. The bone of contention concerned the control of approximately seventeen thousand acres of very fertile canal colony land spread out across 18 villages.[1] The plight of the Okara tenants – who were subjected to considerable state repression that culminated in the use of force by Rangers – was taken up by political parties and human rights organizations, and also garnered a great deal of media coverage. The Okara tenants caused the military considerable embarrassment and arguably opened the floodgates for similar exposés on military high-handedness across the length and breadth of Punjab.

While narratives of social discontent and resistance to the military in Sindh and Balochistan, and to a lesser extent Khyber Pakhtunkhwa, have proliferated over the years, the Okara stand-off was viewed by many as a watershed in so far as it challenged perceptions that rural Punjabis – including those at the bottom of the social hierarchy – enjoy a symbiotic relationship with the state, and the military in particular. We have shown in chapter 2 that a broad state–society consensus was forged by the British colonial regime in

Punjab over a century ago, and that, to a significant extent, this consensus has been relatively durable. However, we have also demonstrated that the military's resource grabbing in the Punjabi heartland, as well as the Siraiki peripheries of the province, is now becoming widespread. In the rest of this chapter, we will provide evidence that the well-known struggle of the tenants of the Okara military farms may in fact just be a microcosm of things to come, as the military's long-cultivated image as the state guardian comes into increasing contradiction with its conduct on the ground.

It would be misleading, however, to suggest that there is, as yet, widespread reaction to the practices that we have outlined in the previous chapter. In fact, a culture of compromise is likely to persist amongst the poor and disenfranchised in rural Punjab. It is only by trying to understand prevalent attitudes that one can make sense of the incidents of resistance that do take place, and the extent to which these incidents foreshadow more substantive and organized efforts to challenge the status quo. Thus, we start the chapter by documenting the persistence of this culture of compromise. In the two sections that follow, we go on to document both covert and overt resistance.

Why Not Resist? Understanding the Culture of Compromise

In thinking about the disinclination of ordinary people in Punjab to confront the military's power in all of its various forms, it is necessary to look back to the basic argument of this book, outlined at length in chapter 2. In so far as the political economy of the Punjab – at least the canal colony and Potohar regions – was built upon a state–society consensus, we have argued that subordinate classes have shared, however little, in the benefits of wealth generation. On the one hand, a large number of Punjabis have been employed in the military profession, or, in more recent times, by autonomous military-owned enterprises. On the other hand, capital investments – made over time in central and northern Punjab, which resulted in the trickle-down of prosperity – have been absent in most other regions of the country.

In effect, this means a general perception of the military as beneficent, since virtually every family in the Punjab is co-opted into a giant web of state and/or quasistate patronage in which military institutions or officers occupy central positions. We have also pointed out, however, that this perception is fracturing somewhat as individual and more systematic examples of abuse of power have started to come to the fore.[2]

Having said this, throughout our time in the field we heard even those respondents who have been subject to this abuse of power lament that they had no option but to tolerate the military's land acquisitions and the personally offensive behavior of military personnel, particularly the Rangers.

We chronicled numerous incidents of flagrant violation of basic human rights which one would expect to induce resistance of some kind. But the prevailing sentiment amongst local communities is that it is better to accept the military's power and accede to its demands rather than risk censure by resisting it.

In Village Lakhiwala in Rahim Yar Khan, the *numberdar* of the village, Chaudhry Akbar Kamboh, told us of an incident where he, along with his two sons, were badly beaten by Rangers at a checkpoint when they refused to allow them to use their motorcycle. The three victims were hospitalized for three days. After being discharged, they made an official complaint to the Rangers' district headquarters, but they were warned that there would be dire consequences if they took their complaints further. When they went to district officials, as well as local politicians, they were told that no one could hold the Rangers to account.

In Bahawalnagar, a young milk-vendor who normally stopped and handed over milk from his containers to Rangers at check posts dared not to do so on a particular day. He was stopped the next time he attempted to cross the same check post and a ruckus ensued. The young man's uncles went to investigate and one (Nawab Watoo) demanded to speak to a commanding officer at the post. He was physically affronted and beaten senseless. The other uncle tried to intervene and eventually both were shot, one fatally. The one we spoke to is crippled for life. He took three shots: one in his left arm, one in the right hand and one in his gut. He has difficulty using either hand.

He subsequently filed cases in the courts for justice, and he informed us that the soldier who fired on him and his brother ostensibly escaped from the Rangers quarter guard, a virtual impossibility without collusion. Three other Rangers present at the time were turned over to the local police and were let off with minor charges. Nawab Wattoo contended that for a while after this event, and during the course of the subsequent investigations, the Rangers were much more circumspect in their dealings with the local community, but they very soon resumed their old ways.

In Tehsil Shakargarh, District Narowal, we met an individual who had his head split open with a large baton simply because he challenged a Rangers official for speaking to him rudely. Perversely, the aggressor cracked his thumb in the process and filed a case against the victim alleging he had been attacked.

These are just some anecdotes that illustrate what ordinary Pakistanis suffer on account of the high-handed behavior of uniformed personnel. We have no doubt that dozens of such abuses of power take place on a daily basis.[3] In almost all such cases, the local courts and police play a dubious role at best – we have already noted that state institutions that ostensibly have a mandate to intervene in the event of abuse of power by military personnel tend not to do so, sometimes sharing in the spoils, but most of the time simply avoiding conflict with the men in khaki.

Lawyers active in district courts confirm this fairly self-evident reality. Many of our informants – who asked for their identities to be kept anonymous – admitted that there is almost no litigation against military personnel in the civil courts because judges either refuse to admit cases or inevitably dismiss petitions for a so-called lack of evidence. There was an interesting episode in Rahim Yar Khan when a lawyer who had represented the Rangers in the past narrated the "official" position of the institution with regard to economic activities that fall outside its legally mandated duties. The lawyer explained that Rangers high up believe that it is necessary to keep their men "engaged" when there is no real threat on and around the border. Moreover, the income generated through so-called productive activities is invested in bettering Rangers' effectiveness as a border security agency. No sooner had this explanation been tendered that other lawyers burst out laughing, exclaiming that everyone knew that income generated from the Rangers' economic adventures went straight into individual pockets. It was left to the lawyer, who was originally pleading the Rangers' case, to sheepishly acknowledge that this was indeed correct.

In Tehsil Khairpur Tamiwali, District Bahawalpur, hundreds of farming households had vacated their lands at the behest of the military under the guise that the latter needed to use the area as a temporary firing-range. Having been assured that they would be able to resume farming their land after the military exercises, the households in question acceded in good faith. The land was subsequently rented out by the military at market rates, some going to military officers. The evictees initiated a court case in 1993, but the formal justice system offered them no respite. Clearly the military felt as if it had established a precedent: we discovered that a file had been moved in the CDA (Cholistan Development Authority) in the summer of 2010 to allocate 145,000 acres of irrigated land for a new firing range in Cholistan.

In another case in the same region, land had been allotted to local people who were due to receive ownership on fulfillment of the terms and conditions of the lease. This land was subsequently allotted to the military for a firing range. A writ was filed in the High Court against the subsequent eviction of the lessees. The soil in question was fertile, the ground water sweet and canal irrigation available. The High Court in the *CDA* v. *Rauf Ghouri* case, concerning 800 allotments on 1600 squares of land, cancelled the military allotments. On appeal, the Supreme Court, which has appellate authority, remanded the case back to the CDA. With retired military officers running the CDA, decisions normally go in favor of the military. Only about one-quarter of the people originally allotted land were able to reclaim it. Many protests and demonstrations have followed and the chief minister was petitioned, but to little avail.

It is important to digress here briefly to consider the extent to which the law of the land protects or disenfranchises working people when they are confronted by an institution of the state engaging in blatant predation. We have noted above that local and even higher courts tend not to take on the military, which can be interpreted simply as the principle of might is right when operating in the intrastate realm. Arguably more disturbing is the fact that the military – alongside other state institutions – can, if need be, invoke formal statutes to evict local communities from both public and private land.

Of particular significance in this regard is the infamous Land Acquisition Act 1894, which provides a mandate for any state institution, including the military, to forcibly resettle sitting populations from any piece of land that is acquired in the name of the proverbial national interest.[1] In the colonial period, this law was employed liberally to commoditize natural resources such as land and forest at the cost of local communities' livelihoods and historic eco-cultural systems. In the postcolonial period, the law has been used conspicuously in the construction of mega water projects; communities living in the vicinity of a proposed dam, canal or reservoir – whether in the zone where construction is planned or in the command area – have, time and again, been forced into involuntary resettlement (Halepoto, 2010). As already mentioned in chapter 3, military personnel have been amongst the more prominent beneficiaries of these mega water projects.[3]

In such an environment where the law actually serves to protect the interests of the state, which is distinct from the interests of the public at large, it is hardly surprising that a majority of ordinary people – in Punjab or anywhere else – would avoid taking on the state. Indeed, as we document in the section on overt resistance, those segments of the rural poor who do challenge the hegemony of the military do so at considerable risk to themselves and their families.

Covert Resistance

Scott (1985) made famous the notion of "everyday acts of resistance," by which he meant incidents of feet-dragging, time-wasting and resource-wasting that did not constitute systemic threats to the established social order but were nevertheless indicative of opposition and dissent to this order. In most cases, such incidents indicate a breakdown of an established moral consensus between rulers and the ruled.

We found numerous instances of local communities engaging in such everyday acts of resistance in lieu of more daring and overt resistance.

As noted in the previous chapter, the stipulation against tree cutting has resulted in a great deal of resentment at almost all of our research sites, particularly given that the Rangers typically contract the cutting of trees to outsiders. In a classic example of covert dissent, many communities have responded by illegally chipping away the barks of trees until they keel over and die. This is an anonymous form of resistance that does not meet with the standard repercussions.

Even more widespread is a language of resistance that is shared across a wide cross-section of society. Unable to voice their intense hatred of military personnel in public, local communities come together and share tales of the cruelty about their aggressors and collectively wish them *buddua* (ill-luck). We heard countless victims of military high-handedness express their disgust privately, even forewarning that if a conflict with a foreign country did ever break out again, they would turn against their own army. A related refrain amongst a group of farmers in Bahawalnagar was:

"If it is our fate to be ruled by a colonial army, the British should never have left because at least they governed based on some law."

In Sialkot there was extraordinarily deep resentment against Rangers, which was evidenced by the use of reference terms such as gangsters and dacoits. As we have discussed in earlier chapters, an antiIndia (antiHindu) state ideology has been cultivated extensively within Punjab, and amongst the most telling comments we heard indicate that the hollowness of this ideology is being exposed – at least in the form of an intensifying idiom of resistance to the military:

"If Islam means what the Rangers are doing to us, we prefer the Hindus to take over our villages because at least they will let us live."

The covert language of resistance is not only damning of military excess but also mocks the military's carefully cultivated image. A lawyer in Bahawalpur was particularly proud of a slogan made popular during the antiMusharraf movement in 2007–8, which captured the prevailing sentiment of ordinary citizens in his district:

"They call themselves Corps Commanders. We call them Chor (Thief) Commanders."[6]

In fact, we found that the resistance of first resort is abusive language. Villagers in Rampura, District Lahore, situated 1.5 km away from the Indian border, maintain cattle to supply milk to Lahore. During fieldwork, while in discussion with a dairy farmer, a Ranger *jawan* (soldier)[7] arrived with empty bottles, filled them with milk and left without even consulting the said villager. The latter, compelled to maintain silence during the episode, spewed out a string of expletives after the milk thief was gone.

Overt Resistance: Incidents of Collective Action

During our research, we observed and heard about spontaneous protests of various kinds in response to the injustices meted out to local communities by both Rangers and other military personnel. The majority of these episodes – a few are highlighted below – do not culminate in any major victory for the affected communities. However, the intensification of overt resistance over time, despite the high costs, does indicate the emergence of a new societal consensus against military excess. Perhaps foreshadowing the future, we document at the end of this section sustained collective action that has resulted in significant benefits accruing to local communities previously subject to blatant abuses of military power.

One of the recurring themes we encountered was of Rangers personnel violating established moral norms of rural Punjab. On a number of occasions we found that local communities respond vociferously to Rangers who openly or secretly spy on women who are active in household or other work. In Bhedian Kalan, a village six kilometers away from the Ganda Singh border in Kasur, the local community's moral outrage was expressed in the form of a major protest on 18 July 2010. Incensed at Rangers personnel who had been ogling women from the roof of a rented house in the village, the local community blocked a main thoroughfare for many hours, raised slogans against the Rangers and demanded justice from the authorities. The event got media coverage (*Daily Times*, 19 July 2010) but there was no immediate action taken on the part of the *tehsil* or district administration.

Another injunction against which there is a fair amount of overt protest is the building of bypasses around cantonment areas, which has resulted in considerable cost and inconvenience to local communities. In Sialkot, the bypass around the cantonment has forced ordinary civilians to travel up to 12 km to reach destinations which are less than 500 yards away. Already furious about this situation, local residents reacted strongly to an arbitrary Rs300 fee charged by the Rangers for a sticker that was necessary to pass through a designated check post. They undertook what was effectively a social boycott and pulled their children out of the Rangers Public School. The Rangers backed down and relinquished their sticker contract, reportedly foregoing almost Rs20 million.

One of the more interesting instances of resistance we came across was in Rahim Yar Khan. A colonel was awarded agricultural land that contained a heritage site in Pathan Hanara. The Buddhist Stupa was about to be bulldozed by the colonel to level the farm, but this was blocked at the last minute by concerned citizens who demonstrated against this action. The endangered site was taken over by the Ministry of Culture and Rs1.8 million awarded for its restoration.

During our visit to Bahawalpur, we came across a major traffic jam caused by road blockades resulting from a large demonstration of farmers protesting water issues in front of the district government offices. We learned later that the procession included about two thousand farmers on motorbikes and ten thousand farmers on foot, which included a large contingent of women. Women were active in confronting the soldiers trying to break up the demonstrations. The head of the Kissan (farmer) Board, the organization responsible for the demonstration, informed us that water was being diverted to a canal (Abasia) that serves the military farms at the expense of a canal (Punjnat) that serves the local farmers. The low water level in Punjnat results in few farmer outlets being served. Records were tampered with by the irrigation department officials to distort reality.

This collective action was successful in that the failure to disperse the demonstrators and the subsequent blockade and paralysis of a major part of the city resulted in the Kissan Board activists being invited in for discussions.[1] The executive engineer agreed to provide an additional 250 cusecs to the Derawar subcanal and 120 cusecs each to the dairy and salary subcanals that serve the farmers.[1] He said this was the maximum he could do given his authority and that more could only be authorized by the chief engineer who happened not to be present on the day of the demonstration. The farmers agreed to disperse that day in view of the partial fulfillment of their demands, but the head of the Kissan Board was fired up and said that this was only the beginning of their fight for social justice in the form of direct action.

In Rakh Azizabad and Rakh Sadiqabad near Chowk Munda in District Rajin Pur, about thirty thousand acres of land was allotted to retired and serving army personnel in 2007. Farmers claimed that this land had been cultivated by their families for more than a century. Once the land was allotted, army men came with the police and started to displace them. Farmers decided to resist the occupation and a dispute ensued. The army officials who managed to gain possession sold it. Others are still trying to claim the land with the support of the police. Two brothers, Muhammad Yusaf and Muhammad Yunis, cultivated a track of land that had been in their family's possession for decades. When they discovered that their land was allotted to a military man, they secured the stay order from the court. However, the army official, accompanied by police, displaced them despite the stay order. Subsequent collective protests by villagers were covered in the newspapers (*Daily Khabrain, Nawa-i Wakt* and *Jang Multan* on 2 July 2008 and the *Daily Dawn* on 20 March 2009).

Unsurprisingly, the most overt and militant forms of resistance to military excess that we observed were in areas close to Okara military farms. Indeed, in both of the cases documented below, local farmers have directly affiliated themselves with the organization founded by the Okara military farms tenants.

In Tehsil Okara, land in seven villages of the so-called Coleyana estate – named for the British Colonel Cole who was allotted 365 squares in the late nineteenth century – has been allotted to ex-servicemen and serving military officers, as well as JCOs and NCOs. However, in 1957, in the initial phase of the General Ayub Khan land reforms, the entire estate was awarded to the *mazareen* (tenants) who had worked the land under the original British allottees. This award was rescinded in 1960 and the land was then allotted, over the next 11 years, to military officials. Land awards were in direct proportion to ranks: JCOs were awarded one square, majors and colonels four squares, and brigadiers and above 10 squares. After 1994, the bulk of the remaining land was allotted to JCOs and NCOs.

All the land was awarded on 10-year leases under a *ghori pal* (horse nurturing) scheme, although many officers were able to get extensions. Tenants who became owners of the land in 1957 were once again relegated to tenant status in 1960. These farmers had been working on the lands for generations and this change in status was a bitter pill to swallow. The military men were expected to manage the land themselves but more than 90 percent of them rented out their allotments.

The resistance over the military allotments started soon after the reallotment process began, and many court cases were initiated, in vain. To add insult to injury, tenants were also confronted with high rents, and arbitrary police mistreatment and evictions when they resisted. In the wake of the successes of the Okara military farms tenants (chapter 7), a new wave of resistance began. The leadership of Okara military farms tenants met with, and directly facilitated, the Coleyana estate farmers. The organizational base subsequently established was able to sustain collective action in the form of a struggle for farmer rights.

Prior to this collective action, farmers who resisted demands for higher rent, ranging from Rs 30,000 to Rs 40,000 per acre, were subject to police evictions initiated by the District Coordinator Officer (DCO). The formation of the union stopped these evictions and rents were reduced from Rs 15,000 to Rs 10,000 per acre, with some farmers refusing to pay even that. As is always the case with collective action, there was some free-riding, such that those not part of the union also benefited from reduced rents. Others who felt intimidated by the state or worried that there would be future consequences continued to pay the higher rents.

The results above were not easily achieved and the struggle for farmers' rights is an ongoing one. Organized groups met with brutal state force. In one such brutal action on March 6 2009, three farmers were killed and 27 wounded while resisting evictions. Agent provocateurs continue to try to undermine the social organization by playing both sides and by trying to create discord – and the leadership receives death threats on their cell phones from "numbers unknown."

Yet, the farmers have been determined in their resistance. The organization elects its office bearers and collects dues from all members that maintain a strike fund. It then covers expenses such as those associated with court cases imposed on farmers, newspaper advertisements for events, support for the lowest income farmers and solidarity events. Women have separate committees; they showed fierce collective action when they mobilized and confronted police with sticks along with the men. In case thugs are used to enforce evictions, farmers have armed themselves. In confronting force, they have also resorted to putting up roadblocks using tractor trolleys.

As in the case of the Okara military farms, prior to the contemporary wave of resistance, farmers were treated with disdain by the military landlords, and their henchmen and women were harassed and did not feel safe. However, since the formation of the union, the tenants demand to be treated with respect and receive their due. The farmers claim to have popular support in their struggle even among middle-income groups in the adjoining towns. Conversely, the military's goodwill had has been severely eroded.

A similar resistance struggle has emerged on the Boyle Gunj military stud farm in Tehsil and District Pakpattan (which borders District Okara). Here, too, the military has controlled the 147 squares of land on the stud farm for over a century, subjecting the tenants who till the land to semiserfdom. In recent times, the tenants have refused to pay rent or surrender harvest shares on 142 of the 147 squares. The more enterprising have claimed a larger share of this land. Both police and Rangers have tried to evict the farmers, unsuccessfully, and the latter have retaliated by destroying the military's greenhouses.

The stud farm was leased from the Government of Punjab by the army at the rate of Rs 110 per acre for 99 years since the second decade of the twentieth century. Initially, share-cropping was in use, but, rather than sharing revenue, as is conventional in such contracts, the army insisted on first netting its expenses from revenues before a division was made, and there was often little left for farmers. The disaffectation of the tenants led to a rental contract at Rs 3,200 per acre in 2003. However, the tenants also found this to be very steep at the time. Many had been evicted from the land in 1972 when the army tried to manage the farm using wage labor. While the old tenants were allowed back after the protests, the current feeling among the tenants is that they have historic rights, dating back to the time of British colonial rule, as cultivators of these lands with more right to it than the military.

Conclusion

We have shown in this chapter that the military continues to get away with high-handed behavior in the Punjab largely because the population accepts arbitrary authority and is willing to compromise rather than suffer the consequences. Notwithstanding the prevalence of this general state of intimidation, we found during our fieldwork a widespread covert form of resistance that suggested that the military had lost its moral authority, become a subject of intense resentment and the butt of scathing comments – *chor* (thief) or *carore* (ten million) commanders replacing corp commanders in popular parlance. More tellingly, on the border, many openly wondered who the enemy was. In addition, we documented both one-time incidents of resistance and sustained collective action by ordinary folk when all recourse had failed. In the following two chapters, we document detailed case studies of overt resistance.

It would be premature to read too much into these narratives of social resentment and resistance. However, they should be a wake-up call for elected representatives to redress obvious imbalances and to ensure that the military serves its constitutional function rather than itself.

Notes

1 Refer to chapter 7 for details about the Okara movement.
2 The larger structural crises in the country are precipitating growing disaffection, even in central Punjab. For example, prolonged electricity load-shedding has paralyzed many of Punjab's small towns and villages and badly affected industrial production. Since the end of the Musharraf dictatorship, the military has insulated itself from the disaffection associated from such structural crises resulting, as they would put it, from civilian incompetence. However, political pundits have pointed out that the pro-Musharraf PML(Q) party in central Punjab lost during the 2008 general election due to voter dissatisfaction with increasing prices and load-shedding. Also, note in table 1.2 the miniscule growth in investment in the power sector by the Musharraf administration relative to the two political administrations that preceded it.
3 In contemporary Balochistan, security agencies – including the Frontier Corps as well as intelligence agencies – have become notorious for "disappearing," torturing and killing Baloch political activists and youth indiscriminately.
4 For the text of the law, see: http://punjablaws.gov.pk/laws/12.html.

5 Punjabi military personnel have historically been allotted a large amount of irrigated lands in upper Sindh, particularly following the construction of the Sukkur and Guddu barrages in the 1930s and 1940s. See Ansari (2005, 28–32).

6 An alternative rendition was "*carore* commanders," where *carore* in local parlance is ten million.

7 The literal translation is young man.

8 The Kissan Board is widely acknowledged to be a front of the Jamaa't-e-Islami (JI). Historically the Kissan Board has tended to take up issues of small and landless peasants in a quite selective manner.

9 A cusec is a measure of flow rate and stands for cubic feet per second.

References

Ansari, S. 2005. *Life After Partition: Migration, Community and Strife in Sindh, 1947–1962.* Karachi: Oxford University Press.

Halepoto, Z. "Water Sector Projects Sans Resettlement Policy." *DAWN*, 14 June 2010.

Scott, J. C. 1985. *Weapons of the Weak: Everyday Acts of Peasant Resistance.* New Haven: Yale University Press.

Chapter Six

BAHRIA TOWN: A MILITARY-RELATED REAL ESTATE VENTURE

Introduction

In June 2012, a scandal involving Arsalan Iftikhar, the son of the Supreme Court chief justice, and the most high-profile property tycoon in Pakistan, Malik Riaz, exploded onto the public radar screen. Malik Riaz's most well-known real estate initiative is the so-called "Bahria Town"[1] housing scheme in the three major metropolitan centers of Islamabad, Rawalpindi and Lahore. This scandal revolved around alleged payments made by Malik Riaz to Arsalan Iftikhar to influence court hearings related to land acquisitions made for the Bahria Town schemes.

Even before Malik Riaz made an appearance at the Supreme Court, Bahria Town executives were diligently trying to clear his name. In what clearly illustrated the link between the military institution and the burgeoning real estate industry, the two most prominent Bahria Town representatives at the Supreme Court were retired major generals Shaukat Sultan and Ehtesham Zamir, formerly director-general of Inter-Services Public Relations (DG-ISPR) and director of Inter-Services Intelligence (DG-ISI). For any ranking general to be embroiled in such a scandal would have been significant news, but for the former heads of the military's public relations wing and its premier intelligence agency to be advocates of the country's biggest business tycoon proved, yet again, that the military is knee deep in corporate initiatives which have nothing to do with its professional – and constitutional – mandate.

While we support public accountability without qualification, our concern here is neither with this particular scandal nor indeed with establishing the extent to which property tycoons such as Malik Riaz exercise influence over state functionaries at the highest level. Instead, following on from chapter 4, we seek to document in this chapter the land-grabbing practices of an ostensibly private sector real estate franchise with links to the military. Bahria Town (Rawalpindi) is alleged to have come into being through the use of significant coercive force to disenfranchise smallholders in periurban areas that have since been accommodated into metropolitan city limits. Following on from chapter 5, we discuss the incidence of resistance to such coercive land-grabbing and the forms that it takes. In the rest of this chapter we start with a brief conceptual discussion of how urban land speculation fits into the broader global political economy and then move on to the case study of Bahria Town.

Conceptual Framework

One of the most prominent aspects of the dominant global political economy since the 1970s – otherwise known as neoliberalism – is the progressive commodification of natural resources. What has been called "financialization" has been based, among other things, on speculative investment in assets such as real estate.[2] While this has meant a tremendous rise in urban land prices, it has also changed the urban landscape itself inasmuch as suburban and even rural lands have been incorporated into the city by reclassifying them as urban. Enormous wealth can be generated by being instrumental and privy to the reclassification (Harvey, 2005).

Large tracts of land previously used for agriculture or even as residential zones in periurban areas have been swallowed up by city developers, and particularly real estate investors. In Pakistani cities, this process has been ongoing since the inception of the Pakistani state itself, and is somewhat unique insofar as most residential quarters in the city –i.e., low- and low-middle-income homes – are built on "illegal" plots of land. These were once used either for agriculture or were classified as wasteland before property developers/speculators recognized the potential windfall gains to be acquired from renting/selling this land to incoming migrants to the city who were unable to afford formal housing quarters (Hasan 1995).[3]

Beyond this longer-term process, however, there has, since the turn of the millennium, been a veritable real estate development binge in Pakistan. Innumerable housing societies have sprung up in all major metropolitan centers catering to a burgeoning urban middle class with money to invest in luxury homes.[1] Importantly for our purposes, these schemes are found in areas that, even until a decade ago, were considered beyond city limits. Both cause and consequence of the expansion of municipal limits, these schemes have caused a massive upsurge in land prices, and more generally resulted in unprecedented fluctuations in land markets.[5]

Schemes such as Bahria Town, along with the more prominent Defense Housing Authority (DHA) – which both draw their names and a significant chunk of personnel from the military –feature forced eviction of villages and periurban settlements that encircle cities. While some owners of land in such areas profit greatly when this land is acquired from them at prevailing market prices by property developers, they are however deprived of the capital gains resulting from the progress of the community. These capital gains are not all taxed away, as George (1886) famously proposed using a "single tax," but mostly privately appropriated. There is also a great deal of evidence, some of which we present in this chapter, to indicate that a much larger number of smallholders are forcibly deprived of their lands –and rights to common property resources – without accruing any meaningful benefit for their troubles.

We show in this chapter that Bahria Town is yet another case among others documented in chapters 4 and 5 in which subaltern and even somewhat well-to-do Punjabis who historically have actively consented to the military's economic, political and cultural dominance find their material and other interests to be in direct contradiction to the institution they once valorized. The fact that the affected population in this case has been historically linked to the main army garrison town of Rawalpindi is significant.

Background: Bahria Town in the Twin Cities

Initiated in 1996, Bahria Town Rawalpindi (the capital Islamabad's twin city) is spread across 40,000 acres and is described by the management as the biggest real estate development in Asia. In any case the scheme is extensive and boasts impressive facilities. It is indeed a very attractive proposition for upwardly mobile Pakistanis who crave first-world residential and leisure amenities.

Bahria Town is a private sector initiative, and a majority of homeowners in the complex are ordinary civilians. But in this way it is not dissimilar to other military-run or affiliated real estate initiatives such as the DHAs which are also formally privately owned and operated and in which a majority of original military allottees do not choose to retain ownership of allotted land. Bahria Town does not of course feature military allottees, but mirrors the DHAs in virtually every other respect, including the presence of retired military officers at the higher levels of management. Needless to say, use of the name "Bahria" – which means Navy – would not have been possible without the approval of the military.[6] Indeed, even if the scheme does not feature military allottees per se, there can be little doubt that its credibility for potential customers and, as we will demonstrate presently, ability of the management to acquire land despite resistance, has much to do with the use of the military name.

The scheme was built on what were then the outskirts of Rawalpindi city on land that was owned by local families, some of which was used for rain-fed agriculture. The Potohar Plateau, of which Rawalpindi is part of, is far from an agriculturally rich region and it was this "underdevelopment" which, as we discussed in chapter 2, explained the British preference of using the area as a military recruitment ground. In the initial period following Bahria Town's incorporation, much was made of the fact that local families would benefit greatly from selling their otherwise unproductive and low-value land into the scheme.

In the event, there were windfall rents for a number of already influential and wealthy landowners in the acquired areas. The rise in prices of land that were coeval with the scheme's initiation and the fact that many of the local people of influence were offered plots following completion of the project ensured that this segment of the "affectee" population, at least, was quite content to support Bahria Town.

As we have already indicated, the scheme has been wildly successful if one is to assume that the thousands of families who have become homeowners in Bahria Town as well as those who were displaced to facilitate the scheme have all benefited from it. However, as we have repeatedly pointed out throughout this book, there have always been losers in the military development projects that have been such a prominent feature of the modern Punjabi landscape. In this case too, the underbelly of perverse development implicates the military in all-too-familiar ways.

Case Study: Death and Displacement in GHQ's Backyard

The particular case study that we highlight in this chapter is broadly representative insofar as huge tracts of land in this and surrounding areas were also acquired through a similar mix of coercion and cooption. The (former) village whose story we tell was located to the west of the Grand Trunk Road, near the Lahore High Court (Rawalpindi Bench) building, and fell within the *mauza* of Kotha Kalan. Remarkably, Bahria Town is only one of at least four housing schemes in the area in which the military is directly or indirectly involved, the others being Askari, DHA and Gulrez. Rawalpindi is also where the military's General Headquarters are located.

Aside from pockets where residences were built, the lands in our case study village, Dhok Bharan, were largely under-used, and were characterized by uneven slopes, rocky terrain and significant ditches. Yet, importantly for the local community, the area included an ancestral graveyard and grazing land was available for livestock.

As in many other villages in the wider Potohar region, the topography made for a very peculiar proprietary pattern insofar as tidbits of land owned by a particular individual or family were interspersed with other tidbits owned by others. This otherwise unusual spatial break-up actually facilitated much of the land-grab that took place, in connivance with local revenue officials.

Our interaction with the villagers in this particular case related to activist work that one of the authors had been doing with squatter settlements in the twin cities of Rawalpindi/Islamabad from the late 1990s. In early 2002, when the residents of Dhok Bharan started to receive eviction notices/threats, contacts were made through a third party to assist in evolving a strategy to resist eviction.

Public rallies and demonstrations took place over a three-month period between January and March 2002 to draw attention to the villagers' predicament, and efforts were made to contact other potential affectees in the surrounding areas.[7] This wider mobilization was obviously not received well within the Bahria Town hierarchy and it was at this point that the true extent of the land grab and the brutal methods being employed became obvious.

Until this point local residents had received messages from the local *patwari* and *tehsildar* (local government revenue officials, see chapter 3) that the Bahria Town administration (until then known in local parlance as a relatively mysterious "investor") wished to purchase their land and were vaguely being offered in the vicinity of Rs 30,000 and Rs 40,000 per *kanal* (one acre is equal to eight *kanals*). This was more or less the open market rate at the time (and was about 5 percent of the open market rate for unbuilt land on the outskirts of Rawalpindi city in summer 2012.

While there were a handful of original land-owners who were quite happy and willing to sell out at the quoted price, a large majority did not wish to.[8] They started to organize protest meetings when the "prodding" of the local revenue officials took the form of intimidation, including threatening phone calls, as well as direct warnings from the *patwari* and *tehsildar* that they would be forcibly stripped of their land – through the manipulation of the revenue record – if they did not accede to the "investor's requests."

It was at this point that the Bahria Town administration's ostensible association with the military started to be invoked freely. The threats being bandied about openly by the local revenue hierarchy started to be augmented by phone calls and "visits" to the local owners by serving and retired military men. The villagers made it clear that the military personnel never approached them in uniforms, and therefore the common perception was that the so-called visitors were low-ranking intelligence officials from Inter Service Intelligence (ISI) or possibly Military Intelligence (MI). Needless to say neither the villagers, nor ourselves, could verify exactly who the visitors were, but it was highly instructive that the latter identified themselves as military personnel to establish the extent of their power.[9]

The threats were, to be sure, interspersed with attempts at cooption as well. There were numerous "incentives" given to the local owners to sell, including commitments that they would be given plots in the new housing scheme.

Tellingly, there were clear attempts to undermine the unity of the village and turn owners against one another. For example, one of the village owners who had earlier committed to selling his land, only to change his mind, ashamedly admitted that he had been initially convinced to sell because he had been told that an equal amount of land adjacent to his own would also have been transferred to his name by local revenue officials in advance of the sale and that he would therefore effectively be earning twice as much. This repentant villager backed out of the agreement because he became convinced that he was going to be swindled by the powerful nexus of revenue officials, military personnel and Bahria Town administrators.

Little did this villager and others know that this nexus was soon to be augmented by gangsters. When the protest meetings and efforts at resisting the forced sale of land reached a fever pitch in March 2002, the intimidation and harassment escalated to a much higher level. We cannot verify the exact date of this incident, but after dusk in late March, armed gangsters entered the village and attacked selected villagers who were considered the leaders of the protest effort. These gangsters were later identified to be operating under the protection of a well-known strongman of the twin cities, Taji Khokhar.[10]

One of the villagers was seriously wounded by gunshots to the stomach, whereas at least two more were also hospitalized. Immediately after the incident the local community came together despite the environment of fear that had been created and attempted to lodge a first information report (FIR) at the local police station. The local station house officer (SHO) at first appeared to be sympathetic and vowed to track down the attackers immediately and take strong punitive action. However, within a few hours it became clear that the police too had already been "bought" by the Taji Khokhar and his accomplices. Indeed, within 24 hours of the attack, an FIR was lodged against a handful of the villagers for attacking their neighbors. The police were attempting to make the entire incident look like a dispute between the villagers, and the involvement of outsiders, including mention of the harassment and intimidation that the villagers had faced from the Bahria Town gang, was completely excluded from any record.

This marked the beginning of the end for the fledgling resistance efforts of the villagers. Within a few short weeks a majority of villagers had agreed to sell their land at whatever rates they were being offered, and it was later established that very few had received even market prices. A handful of villagers held out and their land was eventually subsumed within the scheme, with the revenue officials doctoring sale/purchase agreements and the revenue record so that the resistant villagers were completely disenfranchised. At least one of these victims had vowed to take his case to the superior courts but we are unaware of whether or not he eventually did.[11] With the completion of the Bahria

Town scheme, all record of this village and the means employed to uproot it have been wiped clean, due to the complicity of state officials at all levels.

We want to emphasize again that the military's clout was essential to the successful eviction of villagers, and the subsequent so-called success of the scheme. Bahria Town may nominally be a private initiative, but the reality is that in its conception and genesis the involvement of high-ranking officials of the military was indispensable. Indeed, at a time when the military was directly controlling the reins of government, it can be plausibly argued that the low-ranking revenue officials who actually facilitated the land grab at the local level were also 'encouraged' to do so when they understood that the initiative enjoyed the patronage of military officers at the highest level.

As we have already mentioned, this particular example is not an isolated one. But the very nature of the land grab and the apparently official stamp of authority it has been accorded has prevented public disclosure. It is important to point out here – and this is something we will return to in the concluding chapter – that even when the villagers were trying to protest their impending eviction, the media remained largely unsupportive of their cause. Despite the fact that hundreds and sometimes in excess of a thousand people participated in many of the protest meetings and rallies, coverage of these events was limited at best.

One can only hope that the disclosures that have begun with the eruption of the scandal involving Malik Riaz and the chief justice's son will herald more honest and uncompromising journalistic and political initiatives to bring to account military real estate proprietors and their nonmilitary counterparts. This scandal arguably got more play than it would otherwise have done because, allegedly, some in the media were serving interests that wanted to contain the chief justice's emerging judicial activism. That notwithstanding, our concern is with how the military's widespread economic interests are often at the public's expense, and therefore amount to development denied.

Summary

In chapter 4 we documented rural land grabbing by the military establishment in connivance with, or due to, the subordination of civil authority. In chapter 5, we documented cases of social resistance springing from the social resentment such predatory behavior spawns. The case study documented in this chapter is in a similar vein and demonstrates the extension of the rural land grab to periurban and urban areas. This case study ties into a broader global political economic commodification of the source of peoples' livelihoods. It also demonstrates the enhancement of social inequality since the capital gains forthcoming from the land, rightly owed to the whole community, are privately appropriated, as are the profits. The military's involvement in these real estate schemes have private cover and so are less overt than rural land grabs. Nonetheless, the affected population, sensing the real power behind their displacement, draws the correct conclusion that the guardians are in it for themselves.

Notes

1 Things associated with the Navy are referred to as *Bahria* in local (Urdu) parlance.
2 This commodification in the form of land grabbing has become a world-wide phenomenon in low income countries, particularly in Africa. See Cotula (2012).
3 The illegal squatter settlements that have been constructed in virtually all Pakistani cities in this way are popularly known as *katchi abadis*. Importantly, these settlements cannot come into existence, and survive for decades, without the willing connivance of state functionaries that also share in the profits of the developers/middlemen. By some estimates, 35 percent of Pakistan's total urban population resides in *katchi abadis*.
4 We include in this urban middle class the affluent segments of the Pakistani diaspora, which, in the aftermath of the 11 September 2001 attacks, remitted large amounts of money to Pakistan, often to establish a future home.
5 Siddiqa (2007, 185–99) dedicates considerable space to a discussion of the military's *urban* real estate ventures, but also agrees that schemes such as the Defence Housing Association are built on rural land that is absorbed into city limits.
6 Siddiqa (2007, 177) verifies that the initiative was started as a joint venture between the Navy and a private investor (Malik Riaz) but that relations between the two parties soured and the Navy formally withdrew from the scheme subsequently.
7 At the time the Bahria Town scheme was reaching full throttle and acquisitions of land were taking place, by hook or crook, in all areas that today comprise the project.
8 Our sense, however, is that even those who agreed to sell their lands at the originally quoted price were later turned off by the fact that this quoted price was not matched when they sought to complete the sale transaction.
9 These events were taking place within the first three years of the Musharraf dictatorship, when, with a handful of exceptions (including the Okara movement documented in Chapter 7), the military's power was virtually unchallenged.
10 Taji Khokhar's brother, Nawaz Khokhar, has twice been elected Member of National Assembly (MNA) from the NA-49 (rural) constituency of Islamabad, and was formerly deputy speaker of the National Assembly. The Khokhars are well-established power players in the twin cities, and are especially notorious for land grabbing, particularly in the aftermath of the real estate explosion in 2001. The Khokars' association with Malik Riaz is also well-known, and they have been implicated in some of the many court cases related to forced land acquisition for Bahria Town that have come to the fore in recent years.
11 The recent scandal has brought to light the dozens of individual complaints filed with the courts charging Bahria Town and Malik Riaz with illegal land grabs. See, for example, Nasir Iqbal, "Land Grabbing Cases against Bahria Town SC Bench Facing a Big Task," Dawn.com, http://dawn.com/2012/07/03/land-grabbing-cases-against-bahria-town-sc-bench-facing-a-big-task/.

References

Cotula, L. 2012. *The Great African Land Grab? Agricultural Investments and the Global Food System.* London: Zed Books.

George, H. 1886. *Progress and Poverty.* London: Kegan Paul, Tench & Co.

Harvey, D. 2005. *A Brief History of Neoliberalism.* New York: Oxford University Press.

Hasan, A. 1995. "Informal Settlements and Urban Sustainability in Pakistan." In Robert Bradnock and Glyn Williams (eds), *South Asia in a Globalising World.* Upper Saddle River, NJ: Prentice Hall, 2002, 229–49.

Siddiqa, A. 2007. *Military Inc.: Inside Pakistan's Military Economy.* Karachi: Oxford University Press.

.

Chapter Seven

THE MILITARY AS LANDLORD IN THE PAKISTANI PUNJAB: CASE STUDY OF THE OKARA FARMS[1]

Introduction

Chapter 4 identified palpable social resentment, and chapter 5 highlighted several incidences of social resistance to the military's predatory behavior in the Punjab. The peasant struggle against the military as landlords at the Okara farms has so far garnered the most media and public attention in Pakistan. We explore this case study of social resentment and resistance to the military as landlord in the Punjab, and cast it in the broader context of peasant resistance as a conceptual framework. While some of the historical background of the canal colonies was covered in chapter 2, the specific evolution of the Okara Military Farms in that context is covered below to ensure the case study is self-contained. This enables us to connect this last chapter before the summary with the historical and state theory issues raised as the broad conceptual framework for this book in chapter 2. Tenure relations in the canal colonies and military farms are covered next, with a focus on how contract changes initiated by the military triggered social mobilization. The last sections deal with the actual dispute and peasant revolt.

Conceptual Framework

The wave of peasant studies that proliferated through the 1970s threw up many debates that remain unconcluded and demand further investigation. Among the reasons for this was that such debates simply went out of academic fashion (Shanin 1989).[2] It can also be argued that after the collapse of communism in 1989, radical scholarship in general, and leftist political analysis in particular, experienced a distinct decline, one that undermined peasant studies as well as many other traditions of critical inquiry. A decade and a half after the end of the Cold War, radical critiques of capitalist modernity (Berger 1992; Petras and Veltmeyer 2001, 2003) and its effects on the peasantry are as relevant as they ever have been. Indeed, farmers still comprise over half of humanity, and in one form or another remain the central component of mass protest movements – not just in so-called Third World nations (Brass 1995; Bianco 2001; Washbrook 2007), but also in metropolitan capitalist countries (Bové and Dufour 2001).

Since the 1980s, there has been a dearth of empirical studies that seek to understand the nature of agrarian uprisings in terms of why certain segments of the peasantry may or may not spearhead (or at least participate in) rebellions. Marxist scholarship that has retained an interest in the study of the peasantry and peasant societies – including agrarian revolts – has for the most part retained the well-tried paradigm which conceptualizes a peasantry internally differentiated by class, on the basis of social relations of production. Building on the seminal Marxist framework examining the revolutionary potential of different peasant strata – elaborated initially by Lenin (1964) and subsequently by Mao (1954, 82ff) – a number of later theoretical analyses have looked at the characteristics, the presence and the political role in agrarian movements of rich, middle and poor peasants in a variety of contexts (Wolf 1969; Alavi 1973, 1975; Gough 1968; Ahmad 1977).[3]

Although a universally accepted typology of characteristics that define class differentiation within the peasantry does not exist, the Marxist literature on the subject tends to be consistent in its identification of some broad categories. At the top of the hierarchy are the propertied classes that own or control substantial means of production – especially land – and share political power at the national level. Whilst arguably there are important differences between the categories of capitalist farmer, rich peasant and landlord, the characteristics they have in common are far more significant. In particular, each owns the means of production (land, capital) and exploits the labor-power of others (whether sharecroppers or agricultural workers).[4] At this end of the hierarchy rural property being vastly in excess of subsistence needs means that its owner frequently has to lease holdings in order for cultivation to occur.

The second category is that of the middle peasant, who also owns land but typically does not exploit the labor-power of others. In the case of this particular peasant stratum, provision of basic family subsistence requirements is effected by means of family labor itself. Leaving aside the vexed question of whether the employment of nonwage family labor or paid workers who are also family members is so different from the employment of hired workers from outside the domestic or kinship group, middle peasants are more likely to be exploited (by landlords, rich peasants or merchants) than exploiters (of their own family workers).[5] In good years they survive, to continue as petty commodity producers in the following agricultural cycle. In bad years, by contrast, when crops suffer damage or drought strikes, middle peasants join the ranks of the landless.

The third category, at the bottom of the agrarian class structure, consists of those without property, for whom survival requires they sell their only remaining commodity: the capacity to work for others, for a wage. In many contexts, even these hired laborers are differentiated in terms of access to (*not* ownership of) land. Hence the landless mass or poor peasantry is itself often further subdivided, into sharecropping tenants and wage laborers, depending on the tenure arrangement to which they are subjected.[6]

Are peasants revolutionary?

Where agency is concerned, one influential view is that the small independent peasant proprietor – or the middle peasant – has often played the most revolutionary role in widely varying contexts.[7] Perhaps the most compelling explanation of this fact is that the middle peasant experiences the most tangible decline in living standards as capitalist development proceeds while he (or she) is also the most exposed to urban influences even as this kind of cultivator retains a relationship to the land (Wolf 1988, 371–72). In the case of Pakistani Punjab, there is evidence to suggest a complex interplay of primordial loyalties and class interests that explain why it is the middle peasantry who has most often rebelled against both the local power structure, as represented by landlords and capitalist farmers, and the centralized political authority of the state (Alavi 1973).

At the same time, however, it can be argued that the formulation of the agrarian class structure into poor, middle and rich peasants and capitalist farmers/landlords does not do justice to the far more complex nature of production relations in South Asia (see, for example, Gough 1968, 528–30). Thus it is virtually impossible to delineate exclusive categories of peasant in terms of characteristics that do not simultaneously apply to others. For example, most cultivators – not just rich peasants and landlords – employ wage laborers of one sort or another (particularly on a seasonal basis), and hence can be said to extract surplus value from them. Similarly, middle and rich peasants not only till land that they own but might also rent or work as labor on the land of landlords and/or capitalist farmers.

The analysis presented here, while drawing on insights from the literature mentioned briefly above, is concerned with an unusual peasant revolt in the Pakistani Punjab that began in the year 2000. This agrarian movement has in a short time come to be seen across the entire Pakistani social formation as a symbol of resistance to the postcolonial state dominated by the military. The revolt is unusual in that the peasants are tenants of the state rather than of private landlords. Thus they represent a very small and wholly distinct category of the peasantry not addressed by the framework utilized in the majority of

Marxist analyses. Accordingly, this chapter will first discuss the historical evolution of this kind of peasant, comparing it with other types that have featured prominently in critical scholarship about rural agency. Ultimately, as is the case with the majority of literature on peasant uprisings, the following questions are the ones which most require an answer: why did the agrarian revolt take place, and will it spread further?

In this regard, it is important to note some features of the social structure on state farms in Punjab. First, a small number of the tenants on the Okara military farm could be considered small agrarian capitalists inasmuch as they hire wage labor, sell part of their output for profit, and employ not insignificant amounts of machinery. This is despite the fact that they do not actually own any land. This relatively better-off group of tenants played a significant role in the movement, but was not necessarily its dominant force. The threat of eviction was arguably more acute for the less affluent amongst the tenants and the landless wage laborers, the small agrarian capitalists better equipped to cope with the loss of land. However, it would be difficult to suggest that any one group out of the better-off tenants, the poorer tenants or the landless laborers instigated the tenant revolt. The very fact that all the residents of the farms mobilized collectively to achieve a perceived shared objective suggests that the theoretical approaches referred to above are insufficient to account for the present case.

The second and related point concerns process through which the different classes of peasants/laborers on the state farms developed a collective consciousness. The fact that the authority relation on the farm was far more pronounced between the administration and *all* classes of peasants/laborers than between the peasants/laborers themselves, in spite of the latter not sharing the same class background in terms of relations of production, goes a long way towards explaining the development of a united front against a common adversary. Broadly speaking, all the residents of the farms appeared to associate their livelihood and culture – indeed, their very existence itself – with continued access to land. Their belief that this was, for them, a life or death struggle is encapsulated in the principal slogan of the movemen, '*Malki ya maut*' (literally, 'ownership or death'), a call to action that brought different classes, *quoms* and religious groups together on a common platform.[ii]

Military Farms in Pakistani Punjab: A History

The present revolt centered on the Okara military farms in Pakistani Punjab, a politically sensitive area in the subcontinent long before independence from colonial rule. As indicated in chapter 2, the strategic role of the peasantry in Punjab and the northwest frontier region stemmed from a particular cause, and one that was historically important. It derived from the British imperialist fear that an external invader – specifically Russia – might find willing and powerful internal allies within India itself among discontented peasant proprietors. Hence the necessity for British imperialism to provide an economic and military bulwark, objectives that combined in the concept of a military farm.[9]

This was especially the case after the 1917 Russian Revolution, when the Bolsheviks were seen by the British as an even greater threat than the Tsar, a fear encapsulated in references ('The Punjab peasantry and the Russian menace') to the actual or potential role of the Bolsheviks in promoting and sustaining agrarian unrest.[10] Of significance is the fact that Bolshevik policy was not so much socialist as nationalist, which the British would most certainly have perceived as a threat to their economic and political interests in the region.[11] The resulting discourse ('India for the Indian people') would have been an anticolonial one that proved so effective when deployed subsequently against British rule, not just in India, but also in Malaysia and Africa.

The district of Okara falls within the vast irrigated plains of central Punjab (see figure 7.1) that were the bastion of British colonial power in prepartition India. This area was also the site of a unique historical experiment in imperial social engineering. As indicated in chapter 2, the settlement of the

Figure 7.1. Punjab Districts, circa 1916

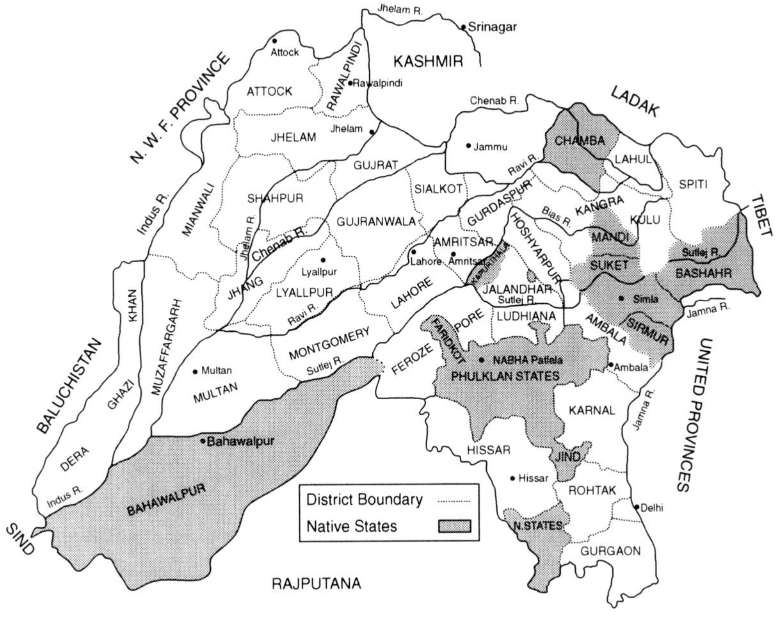

Source: Douie (1916: 223).

canal colonies in the Punjab took place after the establishment of the vast network of irrigation canals in the province by the British during the late nineteenth century. Construction of this canal network, based on perennial irrigation, was not only responsible for turning the western *doabs* from "desert waste" into one of the great centres of commercial agriculture in South Asia, but also for entrenching the structures of power which facilitated British rule throughout the subcontinent (Ali 1988, 3–5). Proof of this latter objective can be found in the way in which the allotment of the newly fertile land was carried out and the promulgation of legislation such as the Punjab Alienation of Land Act 1900, which ensured the use of canal colony land as a means of rewarding those who helped protect British interests and imperial rule over the subcontinent.[12]

Beginning in 1885, a total of nine canal colonies were set up in the Bari, Rechna and Jech *doabs* – the interfluves between the Beas, Sutlej and Ravi rivers, the Ravi and Chenab rivers, and the Chenab and Jhelum Rivers respectively. This process greatly increased the power of the state as it established its ability to confer ownership of land and water resources, thereby giving it *de facto* control over the means of production and the authority to determine the resulting landholding structures. Some significant aspects of the nature and aims of British rule in India were revealed in this colonization process. First, to ensure the continued support of the agricultural castes, the majority of the area was designated for them. The landed and nonlanded elites were similarly won over. Second, a path was paved for an incursion by the military into the land settlement process: on the one hand, land grants for rewarding military service, and on the other hand, production designed specifically for meeting military needs. Invariably, all this took place at the expense of the rural poor and the landless, who were sidelined and excluded from any proprietary share in the new land.

These trends are visible in the settlement of the Lower Bari Doab Colony as well, where Okara is located (see figure 7.2). This colony was settled between 1905 and 1925 and extended over what were then the Montgomery and Multan Districts. The settlement of the Lower Bari Doab met a number of political and economic requirements at the time, and focused primarily on fulfilling military needs (of horse breeding and land grants to military personnel). The distribution of land in the colony between 1914 and 1924 for horse breeding purposes was far in excess of that for any other purpose.[13]

Apart from these horse-breeding grants, "regimental farms and other special objects" fulfilled further military needs. It is within this category that the Military Farms Department received a huge allotment of over twenty thousand acres, known as the Oat Hay Farm (*Ali* 1988, 34). This is estimated to be the largest state farm in the subcontinent. The plan for the Oat Hay

Figure 7.2. Okara in Montgomery District, circa 1916

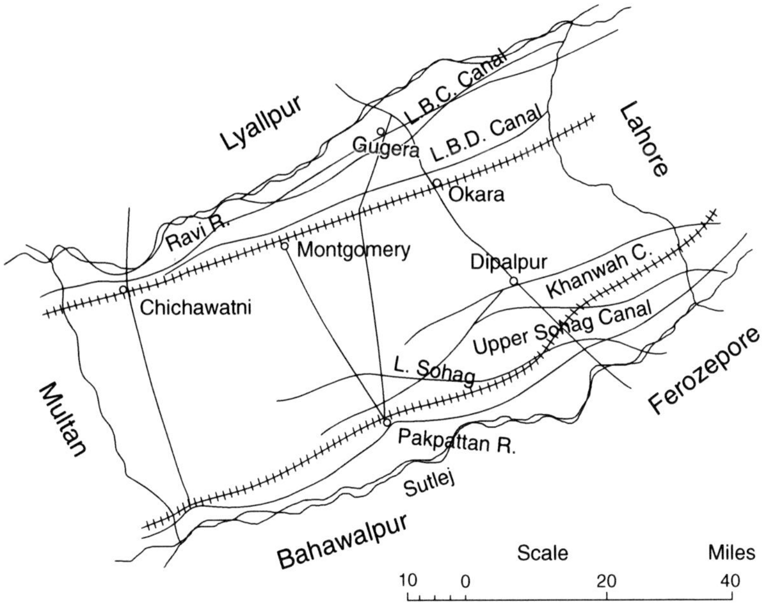

Source: Douie (1916: 263).

Farm, however, dates back to 9 August 1843, as the archives of the India Office Library Records make clear:

> Proposal of the Government of India to make a recurring assignment of Rs. 15,000 per annum to the Punjab Government in consideration of the loss that will be occasioned to Provincial revenues in consequence of the remission of land revenue and *malikana* charges in respect of the land which it is proposed to allot for an oat-hay farm in the Lower Bari Doab Colony.[11]

It was this Oat Hay Farm project that was the predecessor to the present day Military Farms Group Okara. State farms were set up across the prepartition province of Punjab for a variety of needs including agricultural research, although the vast majority of such properties were relatively small in size, at least in comparison to what was to become the Okara military farm. Further, many of the state farms to which the present revolt has spread from Okara have only been acquired by the state relatively recently, typically from private British landowners who remained in Pakistan for a period after 1947. One of the other major sites of the revolt is Pirowal Seed Farm in Khanewal district, a property covering some seven thousand acres that was handed over to the state in 1981 by the British Cotton Growing Association (BCGA).[15]

Tenure Relations in the Canal Colonies

Colonial policy with regard to social relations in the canal colonies was twofold. On the one hand it emphasized the creation of a pliant class of independent peasant proprietors, while on the other it rewarded landlords and state functionaries who had been supportive of the state before and during the 1857 War of Independence.[16] Both groups could be counted upon to provide not only consistent land revenue but also solid political backing to the empire. The second objective was no doubt important, given the British need to establish legitimate and stable rule in the aftermath of the 1857 revolt.

As such, the process through which a category of what were to become peasant proprietors was deliberate. In the first instance, agricultural castes were identified for migration to the canal colony lands, and encouraged to bring their servants (*kammis*) with them, a clear indication of the desire by the state to maintain the existing social hierarchy.[17] There was a clear undertaking then to issue inalienable property rights to the colonists within a stipulated time period, typically ten to fifteen years after initial settlement. In this interim period they had usufruct rights only, and worked on the land as sharecroppers.[18] Meanwhile the landlord class had its already significant economic power augmented by new lands made arable by perennial irrigation (Ali 1988; Gilmartin 1988; Talbot 1988).

Within a relatively short time period, therefore, the British had created what amounted to a new hydraulic society in Central Punjab, one that could and would cater to both its revenue and implicit political needs. By design, property rights to most of the canal colony lands were issued within a relatively short period of time, and a self-reproducing rural hierarchy was established that owed its very existence to the colonial state. The longevity of this social hierarchy depended on the passivity of the nonagricultural *kammis* (traditional artisans) and wage laborers, as it was presumed that the small individual peasant proprietor would not find any reason to challenge the established order. Meanwhile in areas where larger landholdings already existed, the British also reinforced the social order that they encountered when they arrived in the subcontinent.

On those lands that were later to be retained by the state (or commercial agribusiness enterprises such as the BCGA), immigration of agricultural castes was also encouraged under the so-called *abadkari* schemes.[19] In these cases, too, the Raj committed itself to bestowing property rights upon the tillers. However, the promises made to the *abadkars* did not materialize, and they were thus compelled to continue cultivating the land as sharecropping tenants under an arrangement commonly called *battai*. More specifically, they were described as "tenants at will" in the official revenue records, as opposed to occupancy tenants.

On the one hand, the latter were protected against eviction, and were guaranteed ownership within a stipulated time period. On the other hand, "tenants at will" were not protected by any legislation that existed at the time. This was in defiance of official policy, as even special grants such as those made to the military or to the BCGA assumed that tenants cultivating land would be given occupancy rights.[20]

Many of the lands adjacent to state holdings such as Okara military farm were eventually allotted to the colonists, particularly after the creation of Pakistan. Conversely, the tenants of the state continued to be denied property rights to which they were entitled. As "tenants at will" they were also permanently at risk of eviction. All of these factors together meant that the social structure on these farms evolved very differently from the rest of the canal colonies over time. To begin with, there was hardly any distinction within the ranks of tenants along class lines. In other words, every peasant on the state farms was a sharecropper with usufruct rights only, each allotted the same amount of land (typically 25 acres). Over time landholdings did not remain constant, as family size – and especially the number of male heirs – became the determining factor governing landholding area over generations. Nonetheless, in terms of relations of production, the majority of peasants remained sharecropping tenants dependent on the state, which retained ownership of land.

Tenants of state farms lived in villages, and were stratified socially in terms of endogamous *quoms* that have remained intact.[21] Among the variety of cultivators who migrated to the farms were *Jats*, *Arains*, *Cambohs* and *Dogars*. Nor was it necessarily the case that all members of the same caste originally came from the same place. There was also a population of agricultural wage laborers, or *mussallis*. However, unlike the situation on most of the canal colony lands, for the most part *mussallis* earned a living working on land outside the village in which they were resident. This was primarily because the tenants who possessed land often simply could not afford to hire labor.

Other nonagricultural *quoms* – traditional artisans or *kammis* – who were also present on the state farms also had a nonantagonistic relationship with the tenants who cultivated the land. This was because ultimately both the peasants and the *kammis* were subordinate to the farm administration, and thus shared what was a common subordination to one authority. Traditional artisans were relatively few in number, with tenant farmers and landless laborers making up the majority of the village population. In many cases, traditional artisans have either been displaced from their original occupations, or have been able to generate sufficient off-farm income to acquire land outside of the state farms, or even rent land from tenant farmers.[22] On the whole, therefore, the relationship between tenants and *kammis* has remained nonantagonistic, even though historically they had to split what remained of the harvest after the farm administration had taken at least half the crop.

The only meaningful distinction *vis-à-vis* land rights to have emerged on these state farms over time has arisen as a result of intergenerational inheritance. Many descendants of the original tenants either opted for alternative sources of income, or were dispossessed on account of intrafamily disputes; some even agreed to transfer usufruct right to just one sibling. At the same time, prior to the revolt, it was also common for many tenants with small plots of land to supplement their incomes by working as hired labor on privately owned properties on nearby farms. Therefore the category of wage laborer on the state farms includes not just the traditional landless worker – or *mussalli* – but also those tenants or their descendants who now rely mainly on income from selling their labor power as the principal source of livelihood. With the passing of the years, the number of wage laborers has matched or even exceeded the number of tenant farmers. The traditionally landless *mussallis* make up a relatively small proportion of the wage labor class as a whole; the vast majority of hired workers employed on the farms today are either related by blood or marriage to tenant families.

While differences along the lines of *quom* and even class do persist on the state farms, these disparities are in economic terms far less marked than those in the Punjabi villages discussed by Alavi (1973), Ahmad (1977) and Rouse (1983) in their research. Perhaps the only major distinction on the state farms is along religious grounds. Christians in the Punjab were typically converts from the lowest untouchable castes. India under the Raj was heavily influenced by missionaries from the colonizing nation, and there was some provision under the canal colonization schemes to provide land to the "depressed" classes, in which category Christians were accommodated (Ali 1980, 157–71). As such, the Christian community on state farms continues to suffer from discrimination, albeit not overt. Interestingly, virtually all residents of the state farms refer to Christians as a distinct agricultural *quom* – as opposed to *kammi* – reflecting the fact that occupational castes are fluid and can change over time (Ahmad 1977). In spite of the stigma associated with belonging to the Christian community, the fact that all tenants are subordinate to the farm administration has ensured that when the collective interests of the tenants have been threatened, both Christians and Muslims have joined together to form a common front of resistance.

For the most part, residents of the farms were at the mercy of the farm administration that ran these properties almost as if they were private plantations, particularly following the departure of the British. Weddings, funerals and all other social gatherings had to be sanctioned by the administration, while schools, basic health units and other amenities typically provided by the state were not built on the farms until well into the 1980s. The administration accorded preferential treatment to those tenants (or their relatives) that were employed by the administration directly, often using their employees as informers to report on residents of the villages that were involved in suspicious behavior.[23]

Changes in Tenure: The New Contract

In June 2000, the farm management announced that the *battai* arrangement was to be replaced by a new contract system, under which the rent was to be paid in cash rather than by direct division of produce.[24] According to farm officials and the army, this decision was taken to improve the revenue generated from these farms in view of the fall in annual farm income from Rs 40.79 million in 1995–96 to Rs 15.87 million in 1999–2000 (Rs 60 = US$ 1). Whereas these falling revenues are to some degree attributed to corruption within the Military Farm management, the bulk of the blame is put on the economic performance of the tenants.

This is difficult to sustain, given that it was the tenants who had consistently been receiving no more than between a third and a quarter share of the whole produce. Moreover, the chances of malpractice by tenants were next to impossible given the round-the-clock monitoring and supervision by the farm employees. It seems more probable that the farm management itself is responsible for the embezzlement of income and underreporting. According to some senior retired military officers who had been posted in Okara during their years in service, the provision of milk free of cost to officers' households and even the presentation of farm animals from these farms as gifts or bribes to the officers was common practice.

Under the new contract system, tenants would become contract wage laborers for a fixed period, and pay a fixed amount of rent in cash per annum. The lease period was originally set at three years, but later extended to seven years as a concession to the tenants. Seemingly generous, the contract duration is misleading, as the contract itself is subject to annual renewal on the basis of the economic performance during the previous year.[25] The rent at which the land is to be leased out is currently set between a minimum of Rs 2,200 and a maximum of Rs 3,600 per acre. It is estimated that under this system the military farm authorities could earn profits of between Rs 28,170,000 and Rs 46,100,000. Tenants resisted this change mainly because they feared the threat of eviction under this new arrangement. Their fears are based on two clauses in the contract:

> *Clause 11*: If the land is required for defense purposes, the land is to be evacuated at six months' notice. In this case, the contractor will be refunded for the rent already paid by him in advance.

Clause 25: The contractor cannot claim occupancy tenancy rights. Under no circumstances does the contractor possess ownership rights.

Furthermore, the timing of the introduction of this system coincided with the sudden inclusion of some land from *Chak* (village) 11/4-L in the area of military farms and the Okara Cantonment directly cultivated by the army. As a result, some tenant families were dispossessed and displaced. This move by the army to repossess land by evicting those with usufruct rights only served to increase tenant mistrust of the military, and to confirm their worst fears about future developments of the same sort.

The new contract was also unacceptable to tenants on other grounds. For instance, clauses 10 and 13 prohibit the cutting or trimming of trees and digging of mud from a field without prior approval from the farm authorities. Clause 26 of the contract grants ownership rights to the lease holder of only one in every ten trees that he would plant after July 2000, a sharecropping arrangement amount to no more than a tenth of the produce. These are important concerns for tenants who – in the absence of modern amenities such as gas – depend on the trees in their area for the provision of firewood for cooking purposes. Given their poverty, they also depend on the mud from these fields to plaster and repair their *kucha* (mud) houses from time to time. It must be kept in mind that in spite of their long presence on the land, tenants were never allowed by the farm authorities to build any concrete or brick houses in these villages. Thus all these factors, magnified by the threat of eviction, gave an impetus to the formation of a resistance movement as tenants perceived a serious threat not just to their wellbeing but also to their socioeconomic survival as peasants.

While the movement initially started out as a rejection of the contract proposal, once aware that the army itself was neither the legal owner nor the lessee of the land (discussed below), it turned into a struggle for the ownership rights of the land itself. In a matter of months, it spread into nine other districts of Punjab: Multan, Khanewal (Pirowal), Jhang, Sargodha, Pakpattan, Sahiwal, Vihari, Faisalabad and Lahore. All of the land in these districts – amounting to some sixty-eight thousand acres – was leased in the early twentieth century by the Punjab Government to various government departments, including the Ministry of Defense, and is spread over these ten districts (including Okara). The bulk of this land (38.6 percent) is under the control of the armed forces: it accounts for a total of 26,274 acres, corresponding to military farms not just in Okara (17,013 acres) but also in Lahore (6,659 acres), Sargodha (1,525 acres) and Multan (1,050 acres).[26]

The Dispute and the Peasant Revolt

In essence, the dispute over the land on all state farms boils down to the legal status of the state agencies administering the farms. The land for the military farms in Okara was given to the British Indian Army for cultivation under a lease agreement in 1913. While the original lease document is unobtainable, a report by the executive district officer of Okara to the Punjab Board of Revenue attests that the land in question was "transferred by the Government of Punjab to the Central Government (Ministry of Defense) on lease vide Memo No. 1844-S dated 9-8-1913 for a period of 20 years @ 15,000/- per annum for the entire land" (EDOR 2001).

Although this lease was only extended for another five years after 1933, the Ministry of Defense (under British rule) continued to pay rent till 1943. Since the land was in the use of the British Indian Army in 1947, its possession was automatically transferred to the Pakistan Army under the new Ministry of Defense after Partition. Since 1943, the Ministry of Defense has never paid the annual rent to the provincial government.

In this connection, on the 22 September 2001 the Executive District Officer (Revenue) for Okara (EDOR 2001, 1) wrote as follows to the Secretary of the Board of Revenue: "The record of payment of rent/lease money is neither available in this office nor provided by the Military Authorities." Following this, the Board of Revenue asked the deputy director of Military Farm Okara to provide proof of rental payment to the Punjab government for the lease.[27] The failure of the farm management and the army General Headquarters to respond to this query, or even provide any evidence in this regard, further confirms that after 1943 none of the rental payments due were actually paid to the Punjab Government. It also establishes that no attempt has been made by the Ministry of Defense to renew its lease agreement with the provincial government. As such, the Board of Revenue holds that the Ministry of Defense is in illegal occupation of the land in question, for the latter has neither renewed its lease since 1938 nor paid the annual rent to the Punjab government since 1943.

The legal situation on obtaining other farms is similar to that in Okara, in that the lease period under which these government departments were given the land for cultivation has long since expired and the attempt to change the rent collection system from *battai* to contract is being resisted strongly by tenants. All in all, the emergence of this dispute highlights that the Pakistani state still enforces its writ even when in contravention of its own stipulated legal procedures. Furthermore, provincial authorities are powerless to confront the center, and more specifically the army, if and when the latter does subvert due process.

Faced with the prospect of being dispossessed, tenants initially attempted to negotiate their way through the crisis. After the repeated failure of the military farm management to reach an accommodation, tenants expressed their opposition to the unilateral attempt at changing the rent collection system by organizing a peaceful protest. On 7 October 2000 a rally of about a thousand people culminated in a four hour "sit-in" at the lawns of the Deputy Commissioner's Office in Okara (Arif 2003), an event that marked the beginning of the tenant protest movement. Alarmed by this episode, two days later the deputy director of the farms contacted the local police for assistance, alleging that villagers were not allowing the Farm Managers to take away the wood lying in one of the villages (*Chak* 10/4-L). As a result the local police, accompanied by a heavy contingent of the Frontier Constabulary, an Elite Force, raided the village.[28] Here they encountered resistance by women and children from the village, who formed a human barrier to protect their men. Armed only with their *thapas*, these women succeeded in preventing the police from entering their village.[29]

Following this resistance to police harassment, tenants' faith in mass mobilization increased, and gradually they became aware of the fact that they could generate panic within the state machinery simply by virtue of the numbers involved in the movement. There are over one hundred thousand residents of Okara military farms, and typically the movement has been able to mobilize between 30,000 and 40,000 people at any one time. This is despite the fact that less than half of the residents are landholding tenants, or those who are the principal losers as a result of the change in tenure. In other words, the wage laborer has been just as active a participant in the movement as the tenant himself. This is true of other farms as well, where mass mobilization has included many nontenants who have participated actively.[30]

Given this response by the state to the tenants, it is not surprising that the movement has had to rely on civil disobedience, the object being to generate public support by underlining the repressive nature of the state. Tactics have included hunger strikes in urban centers, appeals to international networks, and even foreign missions.[31] The use of mass mobilization to protest peacefully against the state machinery has been remarkably successful, both in attracting public attention and deterring the state from using further coercion to force the tenants into relinquishing their control over the land.[32]

Peasants and the state

It is important to bear in mind that as a distinct strategy, the peasant movement centered on the Okara military farms has refused to invoke the law in its support.[33] This is because the legal code prevailing in Pakistan is virtually indistinguishable from that of the British Raj. As such, many laws serve an expressly colonial mandate. Significantly, the fact that the state refuses to adhere even to colonial laws indicates how tenuous is the notion of legitimacy, not just that associated with the social contract but also that which currently binds state and citizen. Clearly, the Pakistani state still views tenants as subjects, and applies legal provisions selectively to deprive them of basic rights due them as citizens of a notional democratic system.[34]

Whereas initial resistance by petty commodity producers was based on their perception of the protection offered to them by tenancy laws, the agrarian movement has since evolved, to the extent that – in the light of its malleability – tenants now openly question the nature of the law itself. Of particular interest is that tenants have directly confronted the claim of the Pakistani state to dictate what is in the national interest and then codify it under law. This is in keeping with the thesis propounded by Alavi (1975): namely, that on account of its colonial experience, the state apparatus of newly independent nations was not, and could not be, an institution through which a single class exercised political power.

This was because, unlike in European countries, where an indigenous bourgeois rose to power economically and shaped the state apparatus in its own image, in postcolonial societies this task had to some degree already been accomplished by a foreign (metropolitan) bourgeoisie. Hence the state apparatus itself became the crucial site of struggle for economic power exercised in postcolonial contexts (Alavi 1982), as a result of which the so-called bureaucratic-military oligarchy assumed a relatively autonomous role *vis-à-vis* competing interests attempting to wrest control over its project and/or resources (see chapter 2 for more details).

In the final analysis, the challenge by tenants of the Okara military farms amounts to the most important process of questioning the role of the postcolonial state in decades, not least because it no longer puts its faith in prevailing "democratic" institutions. The agrarian movement has been successful in securing its immediate objective: retaining control over the land and maintaining economic security. Tenants have not surrendered harvest shares to the authorities for more than a decade since the beginning of the conflict, thereby gaining economically as well as ideologically from the process of struggle. There is also a new-found sense of dignity and self-respect amongst the residents of the farms that comes from frustrating the state's numerous attempts to enforce a draconian tenure system that peasants were convinced would lead to eviction.

Perhaps more significantly, the tenant movement is perceived as a symbol of the resentment that a majority of Pakistanis feel towards the military and its growing corporate empire, as has also been documented in chapters 4, 5 and 6.

The dominance exercised by the military over state affairs has led to the creation of what amounts to an independent economic interest where this institution is concerned, as evidenced in sectors such as road building, commerce (chapter 4), agriculture (chapter 5), real estate (chapter 6), transport and banking.[35] It is this kind of entrenched institutional power that any challenge to the state apparatus has to confront of necessity.

Peasants and politics

When compared to the peasantry in the canal colonies, tenants on state farms had distinct background and experience in tenure and authority relations. In terms of political awareness, however, peasants on state farms were also caught up in the wave of popular mobilization that accompanied the rise to power of the Pakistan People's Party (PPP) in the 1970 general elections. The peasant mobilizations of the late 1960s, based primarily on calls for land reforms, affected peasants on state farms as dramatically as any other group. Subsequently, as a relatively autonomous (and large) body of petty commodity producers lacking direct patron–client relationships with any established landed elite, state tenants have been able to exercise at least some influence over electoral outcomes. This is particularly so in Okara where the military farm is spread out over seventeen thousand acres and almost twenty villages.

An enhanced political awareness has enabled tenants to lobby amongst the local political elite in Okara and elsewhere, seeking support in their struggle for ownership rights to land.[36] This increased political visibility also explains the tangible increase in delivery of services in tenant villages from the late 1970s onwards, as candidates competing for votes have engaged in "clientelist" practices common in Pakistani politics. Accordingly, until quite recently, farm tenants have remained politically exploitable. This element of political naivety continued even after the movement began. First, tenants were promised ownership rights by two federal ministers on the condition that they voted for General Musharraf in the highly suspect presidential referendum of April 2002, which they did. Second, similar promises were made by an influential Okara landowner, Rao Sikander Iqbal, in the lead up to the October 2002 general election. Following his success, he became federal minister of defense and proceeded to suppress the movement with greater force than was previously employed.

Because of these experiences – an initial radicalization combined with subsequent betrayals by those who promised ownership rights to land – tenants have ceased to place their trust in the state, a factor which explains in part the success of the agrarian revolt. Alienation from the political mainstream has facilitated the development of a distinct consciousness amongst peasants on state farms, not least because the demand for ownership rights brings all the residents of the farms together and places them in opposition to the state. Many leaders of the revolt reveal that while conflicts on the basis of primordial identities were not uncommon prior to the revolt, they almost ceased during the course of the mobilization. It is a subject for future research whether or not the enhanced space generated to challenge established social (gender, class, caste and religious) hierarchies during the peak years of the movement has since shrunk or whether long-term gains have been made by historically oppressed residents of the villages.

Concluding Comment

The case of the Okara military farms as a struggle and revolt is interesting since both state authority and administrative power are concentrated and take the form of state/military as landlord. This has facilitated the evolution of a common political consciousness uniting better-off and poor tenants as well as wage laborers. Differences of *quom*, *biraderi* and religion have not prevented the development of this political consciousness, even if some of the tensions latent on the farms, particularly between the Muslim majority and the Christian community, are still apparent in daily life. In short, tenants, nontenants and even laborers have all united in common opposition to the state/military as landlord, not on the basis of a common class or nonclass position, but rather to form an alliance between classes on a common platform. The reason for this is that all these categories have been affected – both positively and negatively – by the agrarian movement and the state response.

Tenants now retain the entire harvest and therefore have clearly benefited from their participation in the agrarian movement. Similarly, many laborers have started working on the lands of tenants as opposed to private farms, and currently receive a higher wage than that previously earned. Furthermore, as economic independence increases on the farms on the whole, nontenants – including wage laborers – have taken advantage of new economic opportunities generated by the enhanced purchasing power of tenants.[37] Many of those who are not themselves tenants and who have earned significantly from off-farm employment – including overseas – have rented land from existing tenants who have larger plots, and may be unable to cultivate the land with family labor, or no longer have access to inputs from the state.

The latter situation is not uncommon, given that since the beginning of the revolt farm authorities have stopped providing inputs to tenants, and in some instances this was the only arrangement under which peasants could afford to cultivate the small plots they had leased. Many of those who were not tenants nevertheless shared with the latter the full effects of state repression.

Nontenants living on the farms were severely restricted by the siege of the farms conducted by the state, and their livelihoods were correspondingly undermined. As a result, those in this particular category also supported the agrarian revolt, seeing it as a method of restoring the stability and mobility that the actions of the state had made impossible.

Another reason why nontenants have established solidarity with farm tenants, to the extent of sharing a common political consciousness with them, is due to the presence of socioeconomic ties within the villages. Tenants and nontenants alike concur that the latter were clearly economically better off than they had been prior to the revolt, an economic bond strengthened by the fact that currently both groups are beneficiaries of an overall improvement in the village economy. As expected, however, tenants have experienced a much more significant improvement in their material standard of living.

The conditions that gave rise to the revolt on the state farms cannot be replicated in the case of the rural Punjabi social formation at large. This element of specificity notwithstanding, the current agrarian revolt has indeed had a major impact on the prevailing political discourse. It is important not to overemphasize this, however, since there is little to suggest that an organized uprising within the peasantry is an imminent possibility. While it can be argued that the objective conditions for such an uprising exist, it is also the case that the political environment is not conducive. Nonetheless, there are other examples of social resistance mentioned in chapter 5 that clearly got their inspiration from the Okara peasant revolt.

This case study thus established in detail the high handed behavior of the state/military towards the weak and the surprising resistance that was eventually forthcoming. More surprising was the success of this resistance and the inspiration it provided more widely. It also demonstrates another critical point flagged in chapter 2: the high-handed behavior of the military towards civilian institutions. As mentioned in chapter 2 when discussing state theory in the context of Pakistan's political history, when the military is not overtly the state, as is the case during periods of martial law, civilian state institutions function at its behest and to accommodate it.

Notes

1 This chapter has drawn on a 2006 article published by Aasim Sajjad Akhtar in *The Journal of Peasant Studies* 33 (3), 479–501. This chapter benefited from comments on an earlier draft by Asha Amirali and invaluable research assistance from Ayesha Kariapper.

2 Alternatively, it might simply be that the debates themselves changed. This is certainly true of the way that the academic focus on studying the peasantry and peasant society (historical and actual) shifted during the 1980s away from a concern with economic development and towards a near obsession with peasant culture.

3 See also Shanin (1966) for a non-Marxist approach to the same question.

4 In many rural contexts, these same three categories – capitalist farmer, rich peasant and landlord – also combine trading and money lending activities, advancing both commodities and loans to those they employ.

5 There is a non-Marxist concept of exploitation that was applied by the Russian neopopulist theoretician Chayanov (1966) to the peasant family farm, according to which household members are said to be engaged in "self-exploitation." This stems from the need of productive members of the peasant family to work hard in order provide nonproductive members (the very young, the very old) with subsistence provision.

6 Within the category of wage laborers, Ahmad (1973) emphasized the need to consider the large number of nonagricultural workers including traditional artisans.

7 Most analyses have concluded this with a qualification – that the poor peasantry (sharecroppers, wage laborers) has also developed revolutionary tendencies but only after the initial break with the system was instigated by the middle peasantry.

8 This mobilizing slogan deployed by tenants against the landlord is almost exactly the same as that deployed by tenants – *tierra o muerte* ("land or death") – on the large rural estates in the eastern lowlands of Peru some forty years ago (Blanco 1972).

9 Colonial discourse made an explicit link between the retention of the Indian Empire and the continued economic wellbeing of Britain itself, albeit presented in terms of a benign concern for its Indian subjects. Hence the forthright words written by a high-ranking British officer who lectured about fighting on the northwest frontier of India (Villiers-Stuart 1925, 1): "The first thing you want to grasp is that the defense of the Indian Frontier is an Imperial and not a local matter. There are [...] outstanding reasons for that. It is not a case of preserving the gentlemen of "India for the Indians" type from having his mouth shut and his jugular vein opened by a border knife. Firstly, there are several hundred millions of good honest and very pleasant simple people in India whom we are pledged to protect. Secondly, India, if not our best customer economically, is something very near it."

10 On the perceived threat to India from the Bolsheviks, see Villiers-Stuart (1926, 1). Under the rubric of "the Punjab peasantry and the Russian menace," one noted colonial administrator (Trevaskis 1928, 343) wrote: "Like the Roman Empire the British Empire in India was engaged in the forcible urbanization of an unwilling peasantry. But in India the urban civilization was not solely dependent on the peasant armies of the country for the maintenance of its supremacy, and the [1857] Mutiny had shown the helplessness of an Indian peasant army against British skill and military tradition. But a disloyal army might still be dangerous, were India invaded by a foreign foe, especially if the Frontier peasantry were also in a state of discontent. And the growl of the Russian bear now sounded ominously from beyond the Hindu Kush, arousing the British, if not the Indian, Government to a sense of the seriousness of the situation."

11 This much is clear both from the Congress of the Peoples of the East, summoned by the Second Congress of the Communist International and held in Baku during 1920 (Pearce 1977), and from "Theses on the Eastern Question," drawn up in 1922 by its Fourth Congress (contained in Adler 1980, 409ff), which highlight the fact that struggles in India (and other countries) were *national* struggles aimed at European imperialism.

12 The object of the 1900 Punjab Alienation of Land Act was to prevent holdings from being transferred by indebted proprietors to moneylenders in settlement of debts. According to Barrier (1966), during the late nineteenth century the prevalence of

laissez faire economic theory prevented either rural indebtedness or land transfers from being raised as a political issue by the British colonial authorities. The authorities, however, were becoming increasingly concerned lest the acquisition by moneylenders of peasant holdings as a result of debt (Trevaskis 1928, 279; 1931, 24ff; 1932, 59ff) generate agrarian unrest throughout India that would ultimately threaten British imperialism itself. This is evident, for example, from what Sir James Douie wrote about Montgomery district a short while after, where fear of rural unrest combines with the spelling out of its consequences. He notes (1916, 263): "The peasantry [in Montgomery district] belongs largely to various tribes described vaguely as Jats. The most important are Káthias, Wattús, and Kharrals. The last gave trouble in 1857 and were severely punished."

13 The logic of this process is outlined by Trevaskis (1931, 278): "Colonization was well under weigh [sic] when the outbreak of the South African War in 1899 brought the needs of the army vividly to the fore. It was feared that, if ever India became involved in a great war, the supply of horse, mule and camel might fail. Accordingly it was proposed that land should be given to those who would undertake to maintain mares or camels for breeding. This object was dominant in the Lower Jhelum and Lower Bari Doab Canal Colonies, and in the former over 200,000 acres were given out on horse-breeding conditions." The shortcomings of this arrangement are noted by the same source (Trevaskis 1931, 279): 'In the Lower Jhelum Canal Colony, which is based upon the horse-breeding grant, the grantees have been tied down to a system of primogeniture, which is entirely foreign to the Punjab [...] This colony is seriously handicapped by the fact that the conditions imposed by the Government of India in the supposed interests of horse-breeding are detrimental not only to good agriculture but also to good administration, while at the same time inflicting a heavy tax on the resources of the Province. The increased value which the land would acquire if these burdensome conditions were removed would suffice to pay many times over for the establishment of a large Governmental estate devoted to horse-breeding alone. The definite refusal of the Government of India to release the occupants from these onerous conditions is typical of the Simla bureaucracy at its worst."

14 Board of Revenue, 301/2/24/51, Office of the Financial Commissioner, Lahore.

15 The BCGA was a commercial organization that had a presence in most of the British colonies in the aftermath of the American civil war and the so-called "cotton famine" that it gave rise to. During the mid-1920s research conducted into the food consumption patterns of tenants on a farm owned by the BCGA (Lal 1935) revealed a number of significant findings. First, that the association farm, held on a sixty year lease from the State, covered 7,289 acres, on a third of which cotton and wheat were grown on rotation. Second, that BCGA and tenants shared the cost of picking the cotton, which the latter were then required to sell to the former (Lal 1935, 1). Third, that at this period tenants also paid half of the grain produced to the association as rent, plus a further 10 percent for seed (Lal 1935, 15ff). Fourth, that cultivating tenants "appear to be in debt, since the farm books show that they often have to sell produce to the Farm in payment of debts. From May to October they usually have wheat in stock, or borrow from the Farm, and thus their consumption is normal, but for the remainder of the year they may have to omit a meal, or even two meals, and some of the family have to go short at such meals as there are" (Lal, 1935, 14, 112ff). Fifth, that even after rental deductions, better-off tenants retained a marketable surplus, sold by them locally. During the colonial era Okara was an important wheat market, particularly for improved varieties.

In the decade 1925–35, for example, wheat covered some 468, 220 acres, or one third of the crop area in that location (Mahendru 1937, 13–14).

16 Or the Indian Mutiny, as the British termed this event.

17 Family budget data about tenant-cultivators in Lyallpur District during the mid-1930s on the gender division of labor plus on-farm and off-farm employment (Singh and Singh 1937, 33) indicates that at that conjuncture around 60 percent of the annual workload for males in the household was allocated internally, to cultivation of the tenant holding. No female household member spent time on this kind of work, but a relatively large quantity of time (fluctuating between 16 and 49 percent of annual workload) was taken up by off-farm paid work, compared with a much lower figure (between 1 and 3 percent) for males.

18 Policy on land tenures in the canal colonies evolved over time and initially proprietary rights were not guaranteed. It was only after recommendations submitted by the Colonies Committee in 1908 that proprietary rights started to be awarded to the majority of tenants.

19 Grants in this category were made up to 50 acres. There were also yeoman grants (50 to 150 acres) and capitalist grants (150 to 600 acres)

20 Where the state did not bestow proprietary rights upon the grantee, the latter was prohibited by law to sub-let land to a third party.

21 *Quom* is being used here in the tradition of Ahmad (1977), who asserts the complex nature of social hierarchy in a Punjabi village, emphasizing the conjunction of concrete relations of production and occupational caste or *beraderi* (patrilineal lineage) in the evolution of social structure.

22 For example, *Machis* who used to fetch water for the village no longer do so as there is now a comprehensive water supply system in the village replete with taps in every household.

23 The administration needed *chowkidars* (guards), village headmen drivers, cleaners, etc.

24 The information in this and the following section is drawn in large part from Kariapper (2004).

25 In many respects, this contractual change on the Okara Military farms is in keeping with the way employment generally is being transformed throughout the global economy. Under neoliberal capitalist conditions those previously in secure jobs have to apply for their own posts, demonstrating to their employer that they are able to do the same work more efficiently and for less cost than other potential applicants.

26 Some of the other government departments administering these state farms include the Punjab Seed Corporation (in Pirowal, Khanewal), the Maize and Cotton Research Departments (in Sahiwal), the Rice Research Department (in Lahore and Faisalabad) and the Livestock Department (in Sargodha and Sahiwal).

27 This memorandum was dated 4 October 2001.

28 Using a force from another province is again a continuation of a British colonial tradition.

29 These are small, blunt wooden sticks used to wash clothes. They have quickly evolved into the symbol of the movement.

30 Six people have been killed by the authorities over the course of five years since the movement began, and only two were actually tenants, while the rest were wage laborers. These deaths have taken place in direct confrontations with paramilitary forces. On at least three occasions, the Okara farms have been besieged and phone and electricity lines severed. The Pirowal farms have also suffered similar treatment.

There have also been hundreds of criminal cases lodged against the tenants, some on trumped-up charges of antistate sedition and terrorism. Dozens of activists and their supporters have been jailed and many still suffer through the ignominy of regular court appearances.

31 In many respects, the same tactics deployed by the Zapatistas in Chiapas after the peasant uprising of 1994 ensured their survival when confronted by the Mexican state and its army (Washbrook 2007).

32 A prominent New York–based group, Human Rights Watch, condemned the state repression against the tenants in a damning report (HRW 2004).

33 Individual or small groups of tenants may have approached the courts, but this practice too has virtually stopped following the movement's successes.

34 The relationship between the center and the province also suggests that the state operates very much like its centralized predecessor. The state is dominated by the military, this being both the cause and effect of a complete absence of bourgeois democratic practice for much of Pakistan's existence.

35 The military is the country's most powerful land mafia, grabbing prime agricultural and residential lands all over the country, often under the guise of "national interest" (see chapter 6).

36 This has been less the case on the smaller state farms where the tenant populations are considerably smaller.

37 These could include small mechanic shops for which there is now a demand, as more tenants are buying machinery – including tractors and motorcycles.

References

Adler, A. (ed.). 1980. *Theses, Resolutions and Manifestos of the First Four Congresses of the Third International.* London: Ink Links.

Ahmad, S. 1977. *Class and Power in a Punjabi Village.* New York: Monthly Review Press.

Ahmad S. 1973. "Peasant Classes in Pakistan." In K. Gough and H. P. Sharma (eds), *Imperialism and Revolution in South Asia.* New York: Monthly Review Press.

Alavi, H. 1982 [1970]. "State and Class under Peripheral Capitalism." In H. Alavi and T. Shanin (eds), *Introduction to the Sociology of "Developing Societies."* London: Macmillan.

Alavi, H. 1975. "India and the Colonial Mode of Production." In R. Miliband and J. Saville (eds), *The Socialist Register 1975,* London: The Merlin Press.

Alavi, H. 1973a. "Peasants and Revolution." In K. Gough and H. P. Sharma (eds), *Imperialism and Revolution in South Asia.* New York: Monthly Review Press.

Alavi, H. 1973b. "Peasant Classes and Primordial Loyalties." *Journal of Peasant Studies* 1 (1), 23–62.

Ali, I. 1988. *The Punjab under Imperialism.* Oxford: Oxford University Press.

Ali, I., 1980 "The Punjab Canal Colonies, 1885–1940." PhD thesis, Australian National University, Canberra.

Arif, M. 2002. *Jaag Utha Kisaan* [the farmer speaks out]. Islamabad: The Network.

Barrier, N. G. 1966. *The Punjab Alienation of Land Bill of 1900.* Durham, NC: Duke University (Programme in Comparative Studies on Southern Asia, Commonwealth Studies Centre).

Bianco, L. 2001. *Peasants without the Party: Grassroots Movements in Twentieth Century China.* Armonk, NY: M. E. Sharpe.

Berger, G. 1992. *Social Structure and Rural Development in the Third World*. Cambridge: Cambridge University Press.

Blanco, H. 1972. *Land or Death: The Peasant Struggle in Peru*. New York: Pathfinder Press.

Bové, J. and F. Dufour. 2001. *The World is Not for Sale*, London: Verso.

Brass, T (ed.). 1995. *New Farmers' Movements in India*. London: Frank Cass Publishers.

Chayanov, A. V. 1966. *The Theory of Peasant Economy* (edited by D. Thorner, B. Kerblay and R. E. F. Smith). Homewood, IL: Irwin for The American Economic Association.

Douie, J. 1916. *The Punjab, North-West Frontier Province and Kashmir*. London: Cambridge University Press.

Gilmartin, D. 1988. *Empire and Islam*, Berkeley: University of California Press.

Gough, K. 1968. "Peasant Resistance and Revolt in South India." *Pacific Affairs* 41 (4), 526–44.

Gough, K. 1973. "Harijans in Thanjvur." In K. Gough and H. P. Sharma (eds), *Imperialism and Revolution in South Asia*. New York: Monthly Review Press.

Human Rights Watch (HRW). 2004. *Soiled Hands: The Pakistan Army's Repression of the Punjab Farmers' Movement*. New York: HRW.

Kariapper, A. S. 2004. "The Tenants' Movement on the Okara Military Farms." Unpublished thesis, Lahore University of Management Sciences.

Lal, S. 1935. "Rates of Food Consumption by 71 Families of Tenant-Cultivators in the Khanewal Tahsil, Multan District." Publication No. 29. Lahore: Board of Economic Inquiry, Punjab.

Lenin, V. I.. 1964 [1899]. "The Development of Capitalism in Russia." *Collected Works*, vol. 3. Moscow: Foreign Languages Publishing House.

Mahendru, I. D. 1937. *Some Factors Affecting the Price of Wheat in the Punjab*. Publication No. 49. Lahore: Board of Economic Inquiry, Punjab.

Omvedt, G. 1989. "Class, Caste and Land in India." In J. Harriss and H. Alavi (eds), *Sociology of "Developing Societies": South Asia*. Basingstoke: Macmillan Press.

Pearce, B. 1977. *Congress of the Peoples of the East: Baku, September 1920*, London: New Park Publications.

Petras, James and Henry Veltmeyer. 2003. "The Peasantry and the State in Latin America: A Troubled Past, an Uncertain Future." In Tom Brass (ed.), *Latin American Peasants*. Portland, OR: Frank Cass Publishers.

Petras, J. and H. Veltmeyer. 2001. "Are Latin American Peasant Movements Still a Force for Change? Some New Paradigms Revisited." *The Journal of Peasant Studies* 28 (2), 83–118.

Rouse, S. J. 1983. "Systematic Injustice and Inequality: "Maalik" and "Raaiya" in a Punjabi Village." In H. Gardezi J. and Rashid (eds), *Pakistan: The Unstable State*. Lahore: Vanguard Books.

Shanin, T. 1989. *Defining Peasants*. Oxford: Basil Blackwell.

Shanin, T. 1988. ed. *Peasants and Peasant Societies*. Harmondsworth: Penguin.

Shanin, T. 1966. "Peasantry as a Political Factor." *Sociological Review* 14 (1), 5–27.

Singh, L. and A. Singh. 1937. "Family Budgets, 1934-35, of Six Tenant Cultivators in the Lyallpur District." Publication No. 50. Lahore: Board of Economic Inquiry, Punjab.

Talbot, I. 1988. *Punjab and the Raj, 1849–1947*. New Delhi: Manohar Publications.

Trevaskis, H. K. 1932. *The Punjab Today: An Economic Survey of the Punjab in Recent Years (1890–1925)*, vol. 2. Lahore: The 'Civil and Military Gazette' Press.

Trevaskis, H. K. 1931. *The Punjab Today: An Economic Survey of the Punjab in Recent Years (1890–1925)*, vol. 1. Lahore: The 'Civil and Military Gazette' Press.

Trevaskis, H. K. 1928. *The Land of the Five Rivers*, Oxford: Oxford University Press.

Tse-Tung, Mao, 1954, *Selected Works*, vol. 3. London: Lawrence and Wishart.
Villiers-Stuart, C. J. P. 1925. *Letters of a Once Punjab Frontier Force Officer*. London: Sifton Praed & Co., Ltd.
Washbrook, S. (ed.). 2007. *Rural Chiapas Ten Years after the Zapatista Uprising*. London: Routledge.
Wolf E. R. 1988. "On Peasant Rebellions." In T. Shanin (ed.), *Peasants and Peasant Societies*. Harmondsworth: Penguin.
Wolf, E. R., 1969. *Peasant Wars of the Twentieth Century*. New York: Harper and Row.

Intergovernmental correspondence

Executive District Officer Revenue (EDOR), September 9, 2003, Issue of Military Farms Land – Okara (No.45/DOR/TSC), Okara.
District Coordination Officer (DCO), 6 June 2003, the Pirowal Farm Incident, Okara. (No. DOR/TSC/2003/740), Okara.
Board of Revenue (BoR), 13 April 2001, Permanent Transfer of Land Under Stud Farms to Minister of Defense. (D.O. No. 14-2001/631-CL-V), Lahore.
Ministry of Defense, December 1999, [No. F.3/50/99/D-4 (Army-IV)], Rawalpindi.
District Officer Revenue (DOR), June 6, 2003, Minutes of the Meeting of District Price/ Rent Assessment Committee, Okara Held on 12-06-2003 as Required vide Notification No. 2803-2001/24049-CSII Dated 10-10-2001 and No. 1358-2001/1125-CL-II Dated 14-11-2001, Govt. of the Punjab, Colonization Department. (No. 725-3/DOR/ TSC), Okara.
Director General –Inter Services Public Relations (DG-ISPR), 2003, Fact Sheet – Okara Military Farm, Rawalpindi.

Chapter Eight

GUARDIANS NO MORE? THE BREAKDOWN OF THE CONSENSUS

Many Pakistani progressives believe that the so-called Punjabi establishment is the single biggest obstacle to political transformation, and in particular, that the cooption of Punjabis – rich and poor alike – explains in large part the continuing domination of the military. We concur with this view, but with qualifications. First, we have insisted that Punjab cannot be considered a monolith; its geography, economy and society is highly varied, in large part due to the revolutionary changes introduced in certain parts of the province during the colonial period. The distinctions created by the British have been reinforced by the postcolonial state, as well as the differential impact of capitalist development. Second, and relatedly, we have argued that class and other social conflicts have been prominent on Punjab's political landscape throughout the modern period. As the military's voracious resource grabbing has come to the fore, some of these previously latent conflicts have been laid increasingly bare.

While providing a selective summary of our main findings in this concluding chapter, our main focus will be on offering some tentative answers to the following questions that have emerged through the course of our research. First, if the state–society consensus over the military's mythic role is really fracturing, could it be that it only breaks down where ordinary people come face to face with military personnel who are involved in self-aggrandizement (by capturing land and associated resources) and not where there is no direct contact between the military and ordinary people? In other words, is there a duality in the public view between the military as economic actor and the military as guardian of national security? Could it be that those who are resisting or feeling resentment against military land acquisitions distinguish those individual (or groups of) officers with whom they come into contact from the military as an institution? Do those violated still feel that the military is the rightful "guardian of the state?" Without the latter being questioned, can the sociopolitical structure be meaningfully transformed?

These questions take us back to the problem of what constitutes a viable nation-building project. As we stated in chapter 1, authentic development, defined as developing indigenous productive forces, requires a consensus on a common project such that there is collective action and winners either compensate losers via the state or losers identify with the common project and are willing to bear short-term losses. We posit that in the case of Pakistan, this consensus is sorely lacking for two related reasons: first, the so-called ideology of the state – an interpretive scheme adapted from the two nation theory that underpinned Muslim separatism in British India – has been resisted and resented outside the Punjab since the inception of the state; and second, the military's self-anointed role of guardian of the physical and ideological boundaries of the state has precluded the emergence of a genuinely workable democratic alternative to the ideology of the state; one in which all ethnic-national groups and social classes are equally recognized and empowered.

This lack of real democratic voice has allowed the military – with the complicity of other dominant forces – to establish and maintain a stranglehold on power and build a corporate empire. The military has been able to use its power, both while in government and during periods of elected rule, to collectively and individually accumulate a disproportionate share of state resources, which it has directed towards autonomous business initiatives. By disproportionate, we mean both in comparison to other similar services like the civil service, police and judiciary, but also in terms of societal resources. The collective accumulation refers to the quality of life of military officers relative to others when in service and in retirement. The quality of life is both in terms of prime real estate appropriated for cantonments and headquarters (Islamabad being the prime example), and medical, educational services and retirement benefits. Individual accumulation is in terms of entitlements while in service and also retirement benefits. Exclusion thus practiced by the military represents an enhancement of its quality of life at the expense of the rest of the citizenry. Given this exclusion, we refer to this process as development denied.

In particular, the military has consolidated its historical dominance of the rural Punjabi heartland. Yet this dominance has not remained unchallenged. We have attempted to show that even while the military's corporate empire grows, the "traditional" opposition to its political and economic activities from outside Punjab has been augmented by an as yet small but significant challenge from within "the belly of the beast." We have documented the everyday and more overt forms of resistance of relatively poor and politically weak segments of Punjabi society in the last four chapters.

In fact, the resentment and resistance extends to the military's traditional allies. In particular, the military has been high handed with the civilian bureaucracy, at best treating the latter as a junior partner and at worst as incompetent. As early as General Ayub's martial law, military personnel were given preferential access to state resources in comparison to their civilian counterparts. For example, MLR (Martial Law Regulation) 115, clause 10 (1), prohibits government servants from possessing land exceeding one hundred acres, but clause 10 (3) exempts all branches of the military from this restriction (*Land Reforms in Pakistan* (n.d., n.p., 35–36)).

General Musharraf took the militarization of state institutions to unprecedented levels by placing serving generals in charge of all important organizations and institutions including universities and colleges. To add insult to injury, he appointed military monitoring boards, staffed by serving and retired officers, to oversee the functions of the civil bureaucracy. Inevitably, there has been resentment and some push-back. Pakistan's Foreign Service cadre that draws from among the most successful candidates in civil service exams was furious that all ambassador positions were being given to retired generals rather than career diplomats. We confronted fear of the military and a barely concealed resentment at all levels of the bureaucracy. Senior bureaucrats in the government of Punjab were resentful that the land allocation scheme could not even be extended to senior officers of the department (Board of Revenue) that facilitates land allocations for military officers at the request of GHQ. At the district level, we found officers of the Cholistan Development Authority (CDA) viewing military managing directors (MD) of CDA as incapable of understanding and delivering public service.[1]

Other services are equally resentful. An SHO in *Tehsil* Fort Abbas mentioned the thousands of squares of allocations to senior military officers. When we posited that the welfare needs of all institutions that serve the public should be met – including the civil service, police and judiciary, as well as the military – the SHO responded: "some serve and others rule."

The burgeoning tensions between the military and other state institutions are without doubt an important dimension of the evolving story that we have presented here. However, we maintain that the crux of the matter in Pakistan is the perception and practice of working people in Punjab towards the military, and in particular whether or not the teeming opposition to the latter's resource grabbing activities at the local level translate into a challenge to the military's power at the macro level. There is, after all, no evidence to suggest that the other state services, none of which enjoy a reputation for being pro-people, would be willing and/or able in the near future to challenge the military's power, and in the public interest as opposed to their own parochial concerns.

As such, if there is to be a transformation in Pakistan's military-dominated political economy, arguably the most important role will be played by ordinary people and their purported representatives – that is, political parties. It is these that must take the lead in giving the growing societal resentment of the military an overtly political character. Mainstream parties in Pakistan have historically been institutionally weak and politically immature. The incapacity to concede democratic space to a political rival has often facilitated the military's manipulations and eventual takeovers. The military has often used some components of these opportunistic political forces to govern at the expense of arresting the political process and harming the public interest.

We can only hope that political parties are finally willing to push back by drawing strength from social resentment within the belly of the beast, so as to move closer to undoing the so-called consensus. This process has arguably been set in motion by the demand to divide Punjab and create a Siraiki *Suba* (Province), which emerged as a serious issue in Pakistan's political landscape in 2010–11. At the time of writing, all major political parties, including both major factions of the Pakistan Muslim League – which has historically been promilitary and procentre with its electoral roots in northern and central Punjab – have recognized the legitimacy of the Siraiki *Suba* demand and, in some measure, issued support for it.

Such a division of Punjab would confirm our contention that the province is indeed not a monolith that necessarily shares the consensus over security and exclusive religious nationalism. During our fieldwork in the Siraiki areas of the province, particularly in Bahawalpur where much of the recent allotment to the military has taken place, it became clear that a wide cross-section of society craves a change in the existing sociopolitical structure and that the resentment of the Punjabi military runs much deeper than in northern and central Punjab. This is in spite of the fact that many ordinary people are not willing to openly express their political opinions due to an overwhelming military presence and an attendant culture of fear.

Yet there is a growing chorus of voices in the wider Siraiki belt against both military excess and the prevailing administrative arrangement through which power is concentrated in northern and central Punjab, or what Siraikis euphemistically call "Takht Lahore." Siraiki intellectuals and activists feel that this administrative/political arrangement is repressing their distinctive language and ancient and rich culture, since most decisions are taken in the upper Punjab and do not represent their interests. They also find that their Punjabi brethren are more adept in controlling and playing the political process, hence disenfranchising them.[2]

The resentment against the military is so deep that any family whose progeny joined the military before the 1980s is viewed to have "suffered a death in the family." This taboo is said to have been broken of late only because of the settlement of many Punjabis in Bahawalpur and other Siraiki districts which has changed the shape and form of public opinion.

Whether or not the Siraiki *Suba* demand is taken to its logical conclusion by political parties, and how deeply this will affect the overall sociopolitical structure in the country, is dependent also on the role of the media. Historically, the media has towed the so-called official line on India, the military and the political process. Even since the private media "revolution" – which can be said to have taken place during the Musharraf years – there has been no qualitative change in media discourse, even if there is now greater space for dissenting opinion.

So entrenched is this discourse that one of the top English dailies in the country actually lamented the forced retirement of the military officers from the National Accountability Bureau (NAB) in an editorial (*News*, "Bloodletting at NAB," 4 July 2010, 7). While there is undoubtedly political infighting going on, for the *News* to miss the larger picture was a surprise. In fact, the press seems to be unwilling to play a leading role in undoing the "consensus" which reflects greatly on its unspoken political role. In covering a demonstration by the Kissan Board in Bahawalpur against water theft, another leading English language daily, the *Dawn*, completely missed the story or avoided stating that the protest was against the theft of water from the farmers to serve the large allocations to retired military officers (*Dawn*, "Thousand Attend Kissan March," 1 July 2010).

Journalists and scholars often speak of many parts of the Pakistani Punjab as literally being feudal and possessing a feudal culture. It appears perhaps, without being conscious of it, that the military has both literally and symbolically turned into the largest feudal institution in the country.[3] Literally, because of the large land acquisitions by senior military officers, serving and retired; but, more crucially, symbolically, because of its predatory behavior premised on the notion of "might is right."

Resolving this problem requires the strengthening of democratic institutions, and here society faces a chicken and egg or catch-22 conundrum. How can one strengthen democratic institutions without first putting "the military into the barracks"? What except strong democratic institutions can put the military there? Since the restoration of democracy in 2008, the superior judiciary has emerged as another power centre in Pakistani politics, and many seasoned observers, along with ordinary people, believe that the judiciary is the panacea to Pakistan's many problems.

We have written about this prospective new balance of power within the state elsewhere, and particularly the fact that, in this instance, too, the divide between dominant Punjabi public opinion and that of other ethnonational groups remains very much intact.[1] It is important to mention briefly here that the judiciary is, like the military, part of the unelected permanent apparatus. All such institutions must be answerable to the people of Pakistan, as per the social contract that binds the state and the citizenry together. It is another matter that state institutions and the military in particular have denied citizenship rights to many poor and voiceless Pakistanis for much of the country's existence. The judiciary surely has a role to play in establishing the inalienable rights of the Pakistani people, and it can do so only by deferring to the constitutional mandate of the people and their representatives.

In this regard, a new consensus must be generated across a wide cross-section of society to break the destructive cycle of repeated military takeover, and also to ensure balance between the judiciary, parliament and other state institutions. Relatedly, alternative and inclusive ideological foundations need to be constructed, based on a recognition of ethnic diversity, friendly relations with neighboring countries (in particular India), and the privileging of citizens' welfare in resource allocation.

There can be several sources of pressure and several specific steps to strengthen democracy and work toward the dismantling of the national security state. The breakdown of the consensus that we refer to has created the ideal conditions to start the process. The press needs to play a progressive role. The sophistication with which the military has used opportunities to create goodwill and good press for itself has been underestimated. The popular goodwill that the military creates enables it to block any public or private demand for military accountability with impunity, such as placing the Inter Service Intelligence under civilian authority, as should be the case. Extending the accountability of the military to parliament – through the Public Accounts Committee in particular – is a bare minimum first step if the military is to be forced into retreat.

Instead of focusing only on the corruption of politicians and bureaucracy, the press and civil society need to broaden their focus because the rot starts with the military. Instead of being manipulated and allowing the military to play the security state hands-off approach, it should be leading the way towards the demilitarization of civilian life as a first step towards turning the military into an institution that focuses on what it is constitutionally designed to do, i.e., defense, as defined by people's representatives, not on a self-destructive hare-brained conception like "strategic depth."[5]

As civil authority strengthens, military budgetary allocations need to be scrutinized more carefully so that all allocations other than defense readiness get pared down. Most importantly, there need to be consequences for any violation of the constitution by military authorities, and the judiciary will need to stop whitewashing treason. The huge numbers of retired military officers and their welfare will continue to be a challenging issue faced by political authorities, but welfare provision will have to be equitable across society and based on resource constraints the country faces. Ultimately, all roads lead to a struggle for a just peace because this will be a large part of putting the genie back in the bottle.

To sum up, we documented in this book that the consensus on the security state has fractured, and that establishing social justice for a broader social consensus on development will have to start with the military, as Pakistan's most powerful institution and one that arguably sets the tone for the others. Traveling the far reaches of the Punjab, we find no evidence of Pakistan being a failed state. In fact, the military, civil, police and legal institutions work in tandem to ensure law and order based on their own conceptualization of security. This is a state that can deliver. The challenge is to make it deliver social justice rather than social oppression, and that will create a virtuous circle to prosperity.

We believe that development requires collective efforts and sacrifices, but such participation is only likely to be forthcoming if people at large believe the fruits of development are broadly shared, i.e., that social justice prevails. In Pakistan, attaining social justice requires starting with the military. It is the most powerful institution and, as indicated earlier, appropriates the most resources to guarantee its serving and retired staff a first-world lifestyle in terms of health and education, and assets and income for a very comfortable retirement. Since the nature of these appropriations is unjust both in perception and reality, it has set deprivation and social decay in motion that are not reversible until this problem is squarely faced. The military's past and current practice amounts to development denied.

Notes

1 This is not to suggest that the civil bureaucracy in Pakistan has historically been the epitome of public service. Indeed it too has benefited greatly from land allotment schemes that can be traced back to the colonial period. The bureaucracy in Punjab in particular, as is the case with its military counterpart, has enjoyed political and economic power through most of the postcolonial years. However, there is a case to be made for the fact that there is now no longer as much cohesion within the so-called steel frame that was constituted by the British, and that the military's gradual encroachment into all realms of social life is resented even by the civil bureaucracy. See Alavi (1983) and chapter 2 for an account of the shift in power away from the civil bureaucracy towards the military.

2 The greatest resentment is against the regime of General Ayub Khan who initiated the process of military land allocations but, more importantly, who "sold" the Sutlej in the Indus Waters Treaty with India, and literally washed away a riverine civilization that was dependent of the river in exchange for 22,000 cusecs made available via the other Indus tributaries into the canal system. The lack of water in the river is viewed as raising the arsenic level in the soil and hence creating a big increase in arsenic poisoning.

3 We agree with Ahmad (2005) that one can employ the term "feudal" to refer to a particular mode of politics and a set of cultural values reinforced by such politics.

4 See Akhtar (forthcoming).

5 This view ostensibly justifies destructive meddling in Afghan affairs to secure an area of possible retreat in the west if engaged in hostilities to the east.

References

Akhtar, A. S. Forthcoming. "Pakistan's Civil Society Moment and the Democratic Imperative." In G. Pillai (ed.), *The Political Economy of the South Asian Diaspora.* Basingstoke: Palgrave Macmillan

Alavi, H. 1983. "Class and State in Pakistan." In H. Gardezi and J. Rashid (eds). *Pakistan: The Unstable State.* Lahore: Vanguard Books.

Ahmad, E. 2005. "Feudal Culture and Violence." In D. Ahmad, I. Ahmad and Z. Mian (eds), *Between Past and Future: Selected Essays on South Asia by Eqbal Ahmad.* Karachi: Oxford University Press.

GLOSSARY

abadkars	Settlers on former desert land that was made arable by perennial irrigation schemes. Immigrants from other areas who were promised ownership rights.
abadkari	Settlement.
acre	A unit of area used to measure land. One acre is 4046.86 square meters.
Ahmadi	A sect of Islam.
arvi	A root vegetable.
awami	People's.
baddua	Ill-wish.
banjar	Barren.
battai	Sharecropping arrangement whereby the landowner and tenant share input costs as well as the harvest according to a predetermined formula – typically 50/50.
beggar	Labor.
biradari	Commonly used in the Punjab to refer to a patrilineal lineage.
bund	Type of wall used for defense purposes on India–Pakistan border.
carore	Ten million.
chaks	Name given to numerous villages established in the canal colonies under British Raj.
chor	Thief.
Doab	A landmass that falls between two autonomous bodies of water. In this case between any two of Punjab's five rivers.
ghori pal	Horse nurturing.
jawan	Taken literally it means young person, but it is also military jargon for soldier.

jangali	Means the one who lives in forests. People in Punjab who lived in villages along rivers and had very little interaction with cities were called jangalis.
kaai	Used to make rope, paper and cardboard.
kana	A form of bamboo.
kammis	Non-agricultural castes that undertake menial labor. Includes cobblers, barbers, cleaners and agricultural workers.
katcheri	Court.
katchi abadis	Illegal squatter settlements.
khar	Used for making jharus: a broom used for sweeping.
khuls	Openings.
kucha	Flimsy homes built using mud. The opposite of a pucca, which denotes use of solid materials – buildings made with bricks and/or stones and cement.
kissan	Farmer.
malikana	Ownership.
marla	A small unit of area used to measure land. During the British Empire one marla was 160th of an acre.
morcha	Bunker.
murraba	A unit of area used to measure land. One murraba equals 25 acres.
Musallis	A caste of agricultural wage laborers that is considered inferior to the peasant castes. Generally falls into the category of kammis.
mussibat	Trouble.
nallah or nullah	Rivulet.
patwari	An official who keeps land records.
patwari halqa	The area of land under a patwari.
Pathan	A major ethnic group in Pakistan.
qadeem	Old.
qanun go	A land record officer that ranks higher than patwari and lower than tehsil dar.
quom	Commonly used in the Punjab to refer to the occupational caste, although it can have racial and ethnic connotations as well.
rakh	Common land for the grazing of animals.
samosa and pakora	Savories eaten in Pakistan.
suba	Province.
takhat Lahore	Lahore throne.
talwar	A type of curved sword.

tehsil	An administrative division below a district.
tehsil dar	An official in charge of the land records of a tehsil.
thana	Police station.
thappas	A blunt wooden stick used by women in Punjabi villages to wash clothes. It became associated with the resistance movement.
tilor	Game bird.
tirini	Tax.
zamindar	Land owner.

INDEX

Lightning Source UK Ltd.
Milton Keynes UK
UKOW04n0012270215

246965UK00003B/43/P

9 781783 082896